Selling on Shopify

How To Create an Online Store & Profitable eCommerce Business with Shopify

This Shopify guide is perfect for anyone looking to sell products through their own online store, transition an already existing online store to Shopify, or for those seeking an extremely efficient and profitable home business

Are You Ready to Start Selling Online, Today?

By

Brian Patrick
Online Store Owner &
Web Developer/Digital Marketing Consultant

Table of Contents

Introduction

By 2017, retail sales involving the Internet, such as direct eCommerce transactions or as part of a consumers' research, will account for around 60% of retail sales in the U.S. according to a report by Forrester Research Inc. named the "U.S. Cross-Channel Retail Forecast, 2012 To 2017."

Additionally, within 5 years, retail sales made online will almost double from the 5.2% in 2013 to a projected 10.3% (or, $3.6 trillion in eCommerce sales as compared to $370 billion)

The days of shopping in brick and mortar stores are noticeably diminishing. Retail commerce is quickly becoming an online experience, and this outcome stems from both more informed, empowered consumers AND retailers.

Consumers are now armed with mobile devices storing their banking and credit card information so purchases can be made instantly. Consumers have mobile applications designed specifically for comparing prices across all retail stores, both offline and online, and these comparisons include thousands of product reviews from fellow consumers.

Retailers can no longer afford to neglect the wealth of information and technology that their consumers possess. Companies are shifting their resources to meet their customers' fast moving demands for a better online shopping experience. This includes everything from making their online stores more customized for mobile devices, to the creation of e-coupons, to integrating social activity such as Facebook likes in to their product listings.

In the previous two decades (1990-2010), only those companies who could afford to venture online did – and now, these first movers are more than making up for their "risky" venture into eCommerce, in terms of market share and revenue.

In the past, retailers would have to hire large web development firms to build out their online retail technology. With both consumers and projections favoring this shift towards online shopping experiences, more retailers began demanding improved eCommerce technology – and due to this demand, a whole new industry has developed.

Innovative tech and software companies appealing to this demand have begun creating one-size-fits-all software and solutions for retailers across all product categories. These innovations have made it affordable for retailers to meet the new-age demands of their consumers, providing an online shopping experience that their current customers will utilize and future customers will prefer over the brick and mortar experience.

So what does this mean for you?

Well, as a consumer, expect to see a continued shift in retailers catering to your needs through a more integrated, online experience - online storefronts, mobile applications, e-coupons, free shipping incentives online, and so forth.

However, you **did not** grab this book to learn how this shift towards eCommerce will enhance your experience as a consumer.

No.

You realized that because of this shift, new opportunities have arisen within the retail sector and these opportunities are not only accessible to large corporations and retailers like before.

In the past, one needed a commercial retail space, mass inventory, employees, and financing just to enter the retail business. These were considerable barriers to entry, and only those with tons of capital or those willing to risk it all could join the game.

These barriers to entry are almost completely diminished and are no longer prerequisites for venturing into the eCommerce landscape. Today, almost anyone looking to enter the eCommerce industry can – wielding only the little capital it takes to operate a Shopify store and the drive to setup and run the online store (which has a very short learning curve).

Selling Online 101

The influx of innovation within the online retail space has lead to the creation of a variety of platforms and online store solutions for retail businesses and entrepreneurs. This has overwhelmed many of those looking to start selling online, and this ultimately leads to inaction.

You've most likely grabbed a copy of this book because you have decided that you will be using Shopify to create your online store. Both grabbing this book and selecting Shopify for your online store platform were sound decisions!

If Shopify is new to you, don't worry – you will quickly learn how Shopify will not only meet your online selling needs, but far exceed them.

In this section, we will briefly explore all of the available options for those looking to sell online and then we'll discuss why Shopify is the best solution for most online sellers.

Selling on a Third-Party Marketplace

The easiest, and thus most common way to begin selling online is through a third-party marketplace. Third-party marketplaces such as Amazon, Ebay, and Etsy allow sellers to list and sell their products directly from these online stores, rather than from their own store.

For example, an electronics storeowner can create a seller account on Amazon, which would allow him/her to upload their inventory and make it available for sale on Amazon. Tens of thousands of retailers currently utilize third-party marketplaces to sell inventory online, many opting to only use third-party marketplaces to sell their products rather than creating their own online store.

Using a third-party marketplace can be very profitable for many sellers and this is because the marketplace does a lot of the heavy lifting for you. They provide you with the storefront to use, handle taking/processing all the orders, and even market your product to their customers.

Pros of Selling via Third-Party Marketplaces

Quick Setup Process – Can be up and running almost immediately.

Low/No fixed Costs - Only pay commission to the marketplace after a sale is made, a low monthly fee, or both.

Ease of Payment Processing – Payment is usually processed through the marketplace's own payment processer or third-party processor, such as PayPal, making getting paid an easy process.

Increased Visibility & Access to Established Customer Base – Marketplaces want to help market your products because for every sale you make, they get paid their commission.

Cons of Selling via Third-Party Marketplaces

Marketplace Keeps Your Customers – You make the sale, but the marketplace keeps buyers' contact information and will sell them other sellers' products that may or may not be yours.

Paying Commissions – Usually you will pay anywhere between 7-16% of the sale price depending on the marketplace and categorization of product.

Heavy Competition – There are tens of thousands of competing sellers, with many of the sellers having access to the same inventory. This leads to a decrease in pricing, direct pricing wars with other sellers, and thus, only the long established retailers that can operate with small profit margins remain profitable in the long run.

No Control of Customers' Experience - You can only control limited aspects of your products' listings. Also, most marketplaces don't allow or make it hard to offer discounts, coupon codes, and other types of promotions that would help you generate sales.

Not Creating Your Own Business/Brand – You are helping to build the brand of the marketplace and not your own. This makes it very hard to develop a longstanding business and/or sell the business because the customers aren't truly yours and you cannot market new products to them in the future.

Should You Use Third-Party Marketplaces?

Third-party marketplaces provide great opportunities for retailers to increase their revenue and add more profit to their bottom line.

However, there is quite a costly tradeoff involved. You are neither building your own brand nor generating your own customers, and are voluntarily entering a competitive environment full of other sellers (which drives prices down). That being said, third-party marketplaces should be utilized strategically.

Those looking to create a long-term, online selling business should use third-party marketplaces sparingly. Your first priority must be to develop your own store, customer base, and marketing strategy. Once established, you can make your inventory available for sale via the third-party marketplaces.

However, third-party marketplaces do serve as a great testing ground.

Before you decide to buy a bulk order of a new product, or are looking to see which colors of an item sell best, you can place your products on a third-party marketplace where customers already exist. It's much easier to make a few listings on Amazon and/or eBay and tap into their customer base for quick feedback. You can test and track many variables within your listing such as price, product images, descriptions, etc.

Within about a week's time, you will usually have enough sales data from the sales and reporting analytics these marketplaces provide to make a judgment on whether or not you should move forward with the product. If it's a go, you can begin to sell the item on your own online store, more likely at a higher price, and where you can begin collecting customer information, and you're off to the races!

Third-party marketplaces also bode well for online sellers who generally sell a wide variety of products. Those sellers with access to a variety of products may have trouble establishing their own online store. Without having a well-defined customer base, marketing becomes incredibly difficult, making it almost impossible for one to create a successful online store.

Sellers with a wide-ranging inventory should instead look to join as many third-party marketplaces as possible, listing each product on the marketplaces that most likely contain interested buyers of such product.

Third-party marketplaces offer retailers' products great exposure to their massive customer bases, but because so many retailers are being given the same opportunity to list their products, only those sellers that are extremely focused, organized, and have the biggest margins will find long-term success selling on these marketplaces.

Overall, sellers can benefit from the extra exposure, boost in revenue, and opportunities for testing new products that marketplaces provide (just be wary of making your business too reliant on these marketplaces).

This leads us to the next type of opportunity, where retailers looking to sell online can create their own online store.

With everyone looking to join the "eCommerce gold rush", many people begin their journey by utilizing a third-party marketplace to sell products due to the extremely low barrier to entry. As with most things, the easiest is most likely not the best – and this statement holds true in regards to selling online.

Innovation within the eCommerce industry has finally been refined to the point where solutions for non-technical users and storeowners are readily available, empowering us, the "average Joes", with the ability to create world-class online stores that rival those of any Fortune 500 company.

Previous barriers to entry such as retail space, employees, and massive inventory stockpiles no longer exist; the new barriers to entry include just a small monthly fee to run your store and the short span of time it takes to understand how to operate the online store you create.

Let's first take a quick look at the pros and cons of creating your own store before we explore the various solutions made available to you.

Pros of Creating Your Own Online Store

You Are Creating Your Own Business/Brand – Every sale you make generates a new customer for your business that you can re-sell to in the future. From day one, you are creating a valuable, tangible, and sellable asset by building up a list of customers.

No Paying Commissions – Instead of paying 7-16% of every sale to a third-party marketplace, you get to keep every dollar of your sales (minus the small payment processing fee).

No Competition – When you sell your items on the open marketplace, you are competing with thousands of other sellers. Creating your own online store allows you to control pricing of your inventory without having to feel the pressure of competing sellers.

Control of Customer Experience – Having your own store allows for complete control over your customers' experience. You can ask them to interact with you on social media, provide them with sales and discount codes, offer shipping promotions, and collect their email so that you can market to them again.

Cons of Creating Your Own Online Store

Slight Learning Curve – It used to be near impossible to set up an online store without having technical skills, now it's quite easy for most non-technical persons to set up their own their store in just a few hours.

Fixed Cost – Selling on third-party marketplaces usually can be done without having to pay any upfront costs; you only pay commissions on products sold. Creating your own online store will require a small upfront cost or monthly recurring cost, depending on if you host the store yourself (upfront cost) or use an online store creator like Shopify (recurring cost).

*While retail businesses in the past, and most other businesses today, require a fair amount of startup capital, the minimal cost ($10-15/monthly) for setting up your own store is almost laughable.

No Established Customer Base – Since your products are not being placed for sale on already-established marketplaces, you must have a method for driving potential customers to your store. Many people get overwhelmed with the thought of getting visitors to their online store.

While important, there are a million and one ways to get targeted visitors to your website – focus should be placed on market/product research to ensure the offer is in actual demand. Once you have a product/service that people want, getting traffic becomes incredibly simple because you can define this "ideal customer". Then it's just a matter of finding out where these potential customers spend their time online (Facebook, searching on Google, etc.) so that way you can market to them.

*We go over the most efficient marketing methods later on in the book…after you've set up your store!

Should You Create Your Own Online Store

Just because you can create your own store, should you?

Most online sellers should create their own online store.

Period.

A few years back, this may have not been the case, but without almost any barriers to entry, any retailer or individual interested in creating their own online store, should.

As mentioned before, if you are looking at creating a long-term, sustainable online selling business, you must not solely rely on third-party marketplaces. By doing so, you are conceding to someone else's business right from the get-go. This places limits on your business's potential and by linking closely to another business, you greatly endanger your own business and are openly inviting volatility.

Again, there may be opportune times where third-party marketplaces may help you grow your business and reach more customers, but the <u>foundation of your business</u> must be <u>your own</u>

<u>store</u>.

Solutions for Creating Your Own Online Store

A quick search in Google with the terms "create an online store" will bring up most of the reputable and readily available options you have for creating your store. Let's look at an overview of all these solutions to break down exactly what you are being offered to create your store.

All of the results retrieved by such a search can be classified into two types of solutions: Self-Hosted Online Stores & Hosted Online Stores.

Self-Hosted Online Stores

Self-hosted online stores are just that – you host them yourself. You must first have your own website hosting solution in place, which you can set up yourself if technical or purchase from a company like GoDaddy.com for a monthly fee.

With hosting in place, you can begin to build your online store. At this point, you will have two options for building your website.

The first option will be to use a Content Management System (CMS), such as Wordpress or Joomla, which essentially gives you a platform/framework to build your store on top of.

This allows non-technical users the ability to build a website/online store by using previously built templates and functionalities that other users have created. Basically, you will be assembling your store piece by piece. Need shopping cart functionality? You would find a function someone already built and add it to your website. Want to add a way for customers to use discount codes? You would find a function someone already built and add it to your website.

If you are looking at using a CMS to help expedite building your online store, I would highly suggesting using Wordpress. In addition to Wordpress, you should also use designs and functionalities offered by a company called WooCommerce. They specialize in online store templates and functionalities that you can piece together to build your store on top of the Wordpress CMS.

The second option would be to create your online store from the ground up. This would require advanced programming skills and/or outsourcing the work to an experienced programmer for what would be a substantial amount of money.

This option used to make sense in some instances, but due to the rapid advancements made by content management systems like Wordpress, and of course hosted online store builders, which we will discuss next, one should no longer consider this an option.

Hosted Online Stores

The second way you can create your online store is by using a hosted online store solution. Online stores hosted by another company, and not you, are referred to as hosted online stores.

You are ultimately choosing to use a company's online store building services to create your store, and with that decision, you eliminate the need to set up your own web hosting. By paying to use their online store builder, usually a monthly fee, the cost of hosting your store is covered in addition to the various features and functions they provide you with to build your store.

The decision to choose a hosted online store or a self-hosted online store was once a complicated one. Self-hosted online stores provided unlimited flexibility in how you could create your store, from everything to the design to how it functions. Additionally, in previous years, there weren't many companies offering worthwhile solutions for creating a hosted store with them.

However, very recently, new companies have fulfilled this demand for easy-to-use hosted online stores, empowering business owners to create unique and high-powered stores.

Two years ago I built my online stores using my own self-hosted solution combining Wordpress and WooCommerce. Now, due to the rapid advancement in hosted solutions, I exclusively use hosted online store builders (Shopify of course!) to build any of my clients' online stores and my own.

Using a hosted online solution is the undisputable, best solution for 99.99% of those looking to sell online through their own stores (the .01% being Amazon and extremely massive enterprises).

Choosing Your Hosted Online Store Builder

With the distinction between self-hosted and hosted online stores addressed, let's look back to the results that came up with our Google search for "create an online store".

Entering this query into Google will bring about a ton of companies that are all offering their hosted Online Store Builder solution, which is what we are looking for.

With so many online store builders to choose from, and the free trial periods that many offer, many people get caught up in trying them all - only to be left more confused then when they started.

The biggest and "best" solutions currently available, include: BigCommerce, Volusion, 3Dcart, and Shopify.

Again, if you Google the above store builders and/or look for blogs that attempt to distinguish the individual features and benefits of each, you will become "information overloaded" which will lead to inaction.

I've tried every single one of the solutions above, and for the most part, they all do the same thing. BigCommerce and Shopify standout above the rest and lead the pack when it comes to features offered, price, and the ability to create attractive storefronts that also are effective in driving sales.

Where Shopify clearly becomes the best solution, is when you address "ease of use". Within 60 minutes of using Shopify, I was able to create my first online store that was more capable and visually appealing than any other website or store I had ever made, even with my more than eight years in web design.

The real beauty was that I was able to add all of my products and begin marketing to my customers that same day. I was not bogged down with technical components or the common faults usually found with payment processing and adding shipping details. I simply built the store exactly to my liking and went live with it.

That being said, it's time to dive into what Shopify is exactly and how it will help you transition your retail business online or enable you to create a new business as an online seller.

Creating an Online Store with Shopify

Enter Shopify, a simple eCommerce platform that makes it easy for businesses of all sizes to create and operate their own online store. It allows retailers to build and host their own unique eCommerce websites, and it streamlines other functions within an eCommerce business that were once very time consuming.

Shopify was created by small eCommerce entrepreneurs. In 2004, Tobias Lütke, a web developer, started the site with two friends after attempting to build an online marketplace for his snowboarding equipment business. Disappointed with all the site-building software options available to him, Lütke wanted to, in his own words, "spite" the competition, and used open source programming to build the first version of his snowboarding store, sharing the code he used via a new site called Shopify in 2006.

Since 2010, Shopify has pulled in $122 million in funding, according to CrunchBase, and is now used by Forbes, Gatorade, Tesla Motors, Amnesty International, CrossFit, and other companies large and small. According to their website, Shopify has helped create 90,000 online stores, all of which have brought in more than $3 billion in sales together.

Shopify is the best, end-to-end eCommerce solution available today. Not only can you create a beautiful online store in minutes, more importantly, you are given access to every feature you will ever need for actually running your business. Everything from taking orders, to processing payment, to tracking your visitors' actions is handled by Shopify.

Let's take a look at a quick overview of all features provided by Shopify and how each feature helps you create and manage your online store.

Shopify Features Overview

This section is meant for those users looking to learn a little more about Shopify before getting started, or may just be looking for clarification as to what a hosted online store building solution is comprised of. If you are ready to get your store off the ground, head to the next chapter.

Hundreds of Professionally Designed Themes

Shopify offers a wide range of both free and premium "Themes" to use for your store's design. Their free themes are very aesthetically pleasing and also highly effective in terms of driving sales and helping your customers move around your website.

Premium themes allow you to build an even more involved storefront, however, I've never had to enlist a premium theme to meet all of my needs. Most other hosted online store solutions will provide several free "basic" themes that are terrible and will try and upsell you on a premium theme; this is not the case with Shopify.

In addition to selecting one of these themes, you are provided with the ability to create your own theme or completely customize your existing theme. Unlike many other hosted solutions, Shopify does not restrict your ability to customize your store. You can make any HTML & CSS changes needed to completely transform your website's appearance, even though 99% of users will be more than satisfied with the hundreds of templates offered by Shopify and the moveable parts within each one.

Mobile Friendly

Every Shopify theme is mobile commerce enabled. Your online store can accept orders across any device whether it's a tablet, mobile phone, or desktop computer. More and more customers are using their mobile devices to do their online shopping, making this a highly beneficial feature for all Shopify storeowners.

With visitors perusing your store from a wide range of mobile and desktop devices, it is important that your store appears and functions the same no matter where these visitors come from. Shopify's themes are referred to as "responsive" themes, meaning they have been developed to appear properly on any type of device viewing it.

This technology saves you a ton of headache and dollars as online stores used to require separate websites made specifically for every type of device. With Shopify, you build your store once and they'll ensure that it appears correctly on any device at no additional cost.

Hosting, Email, and Domain

As mentioned in the previous chapter, Shopify is a Hosted Online Store, which means they take care of the hosting for your store and related needs.

Hosting

Many hosting providers will increase your monthly billing rate if your site receives more visitors than the allotted plan allows for. This is never the case with Shopify as you will never be charged more for this additional bandwidth.

Shopify's servers are some of the fastest around, so visitors will never have to wait for your website to load. Website loading times may seem irrelevant, but it's one of the most influential factors in delivering a positive shopping experience for your visitors. Shopify delivers blazing fast results because they enlist a CDN, content delivery network, to store your files across a mass network of worldwide servers so your website loads quickly no matter where your customers are visiting from.

Domains

Shopify makes it easy to use your own domain name for your online store. While they do provide you with a free sub-domain (e.g. johnspetstore.myshopify.com), it's encouraged that you register your own domain name for a variety of practical and marketing-related reasons. They can help you find and purchase your domain, or walk you through adjusting a domain you already own so it becomes your store's domain.

Email Forwarding

If you decide to buy a domain from Shopify, you will be able to set up email addresses using the domain's name in them. For example, you can create a bunch of email addresses such as "contact@yourstore.com" and "john@yourstore.com" and have these emails forward to an email account you already own to give you a more professional appearance when communicating with customers and other business owners.

Handling All Administrative Tasks

Within minutes of signing up and selecting your store's theme, you can start taking orders because all of the backend, administrative tasks are taken care of for you – within your Shopify administrator dashboard.

Reporting

You can easily track and analyze all of your orders, sales, and payments – giving you the insight needed to find trends and better your understanding of what customers' needs are. Export any report you need to a spreadsheet for yourself, or even better, to pass it off to your accountant.

Customers

Find your customers' contact information and their order histories from within your Shopify administrator dashboard.

Customers are encouraged to make a quick customer account when checking out on your store, which is a great function, offered by Shopify. This makes it easier for customers to become repeat customers because all of their information is saved and future purchases can be made in an instant.

Payment Processing

One of the best features is Shopify's ability to handle your customers' payments directly. How many times do you find yourself ready to make a purchase online, but then the website takes you to another website or complicates the checkout process?

With Shopify, then entire buying process is streamlined. You can choose to accept payments using Shopify Payments, Shopify's own payment processing system. In the past, you would have to use a payment gateway such as Paypal or Authorize.net to process all of your billing.

If you prefer, you can still sync any of the 70+ payment gateways to your store and handle payment that way.

In addition to online payment processing, you can process orders in person with Shopify Mobile! That's right, you can accept orders from your mobile or tablet device by simply using the Shopify Mobile app. Shopify will even provide you with a Point of Sale (POS) Card Reader so you can swipe customers' cards and quickly complete the transaction in person from your tablet or mobile device.

Checkout Delivery & Functionality

Shopify's checkout process makes the buying process a seamless one, which is crucial to the online retail experience customers now are use to. Customers are taken through the checkout process quickly and securely. Shopify provides your store a FREE 128-bit SSL certification which is required to secure customer information. With other online store builders, this safety encryption usually has to be purchased separately.

Shopify is also certified Level 1 PCI DSS compliant meaning it accepts the major credit cards, allowing pretty much any customer to purchase from your store with ease.

Abandoned Checkout Recovery

Not only does Shopify provide your customers with a great checkout experience, but they also provide you the option to send out emails to prospective customers who've placed products in their online shopping cart, but have not yet completed the order.

This feature is just another example of how Shopify separates itself from other online store builders. This feature has noticeably boosted sales across all of my clients' stores, as well as my own. This feature is only included within certain Shopify accounts.

Shipping & Tax Rates

Shipping rates can be easily managed from your admin dashboard, giving you the ability to set up various rates. For example, you can dictate the shipping rates across your entire store using a fixed-price model (e.g. $5 for shipping within the

U.S. and free shipping for orders over $50) or you can select a weight-based model.

Depending on your account type, Shopify will allow you to utilize their automatic shipping rate functionality so that every order's shipping cost is calculated on the spot and added to your customers' orders. This will ensure that you never take a loss on shipping costs.

Taxes are easily made manageable by Shopify. They automatically calculate the various country and state tax rates for you. You can choose to include these within your products' pricing or add on to your customers' orders with a single setting.

Managing Your Store's Content

Shopify also acts as a content management system (CMS), similar to Wordpress, which we discussed earlier. You can control all of the aspects of your store that your customer sees from your backend dashboard. From the pages, to the product listings, to the blog, to the navigational menu – everything can be completely managed and rearranged with just a few clicks of the mouse.

Blogging

In addition to the pages needed to run an online store, Shopify provides complete blogging functionality so that you can add and manage content across your online store. Everything from adding articles/blog posts on your website to enabling customer comments is a few clicks away. This feature is overlooked by many storeowners, but adding new content to your blog is a great way to get new visitors to your website.

Marketing Features

Shopify again separates itself from other hosted online store solutions by acknowledging the importance of marketing by integrating features that will help you increase the amount of visitors coming to your store.

Search Engine Optimization (SEO)

Search engine optimization (SEO) is the process of increasing a website's visibility so that appears in the search results of a search engine. In layman's terms, the better your online store's SEO is, the higher your website will appear in search results when visitors are looking for products or information related to your business. To help search engines better rank your store for various keyword searches, there are a variety of things a storeowner can do, most of which can be done when logged into your Shopify dashboard.

You will be able to complete the majority of SEO best practices, which include customizing your page titles, adjusting page URLS to include keywords, and adding meta-data to your pages, products, and even images. Shopify even generates an XML Sitemap for you; this is what notifies search engines of the new products and content added to your store on an ongoing basis.

Discount Codes & Gift Cards

Shopify offers a wide variety of promotional tools to help you run promotions and offer discounts to attract new customers and reward returning customers. In your dashboard, you are able to create discount codes that can be redeemed by customers to save them a certain dollar amount, a percentage off the price, or provide them with free shipping.

You can even create gift cards for customers to purchase, and those redeeming the gift card can check their gift card's balance at any point right by visiting a page on your store.

Social Media Integration

All of the Shopify themes allow you to enable integration of social media sites so that customers can share your products with their social networks. This feature will attract new visitors to your store without you having to do any extra work.

Email Marketing Integration

Shopify has made it a priority to integrate with Mailchimp, a leading email marketing company, in order to streamline email marketing efforts. Email marketing is the most powerful marketing tool available today. Email marketing will allow you to send out promotions, share new content, and announce product launches to those customers on your email list.

Advanced Analytics

Advanced marketers rely heavily on data to help them create profitable marketing campaigns and advertisements. Within Shopify's dashboard, you will find a custom analytics platform keeping track of you store's performance so that you can make those critical decisions dictating your businesses' success.

Having these analytics in place allows you to track your various marketing and advertising campaigns, providing you with the data to eliminate poor performing campaigns and expand on those efforts that are actually bringing in profits.

Advanced Functionalities – Shopify App Store

Innovation within the eCommerce space is rapidly evolving, which is why Shopify has created an open source marketplace for developers to offer storeowners new functionalities for their stores in the form of apps.

Shopify apps provide you the ability to enhance your online store by adding new functionalities. Shopify offers the ultimate online store solution, but understands that other developers are better at creating certain functionalities. This gives you the best of both worlds. Shopify provides you with a powerful online store solution, and then you can tap into incredibly powerful applications depending on what you want to add to your store.

New apps are constantly being added to the app store, helping you enhance your store's marketing functionalities, provide advanced tracking/reporting, sync services for 3rd party applications, such as retargeting advertising, and much more.

Customer Support

Shopify offers 24/7 customer phone support, as well as live chatting with representatives online, and a comprehensive library of additional resources, video-tutorials, and FAQs.

While this book serves as a shortcut and customized guide for getting you from start to finish, the database of helpful resources is always worth searching when you have a particular question or are in need of help.

Getting Started with Your Shopify Store

This section will act as your quick starter guide – taking you from opening your Shopify account to a completed, live store that's ready to sell products.

Let's first look at the various account options currently offered by Shopify so you can determine which plan best suits your needs.

Shopify gives you 14 days of free service to start, but at the end of your free trial, you'll have to select a plan. Plans range from $14/month to $179/month, and then you may find variable fees depending on the payment processor you choose or if you utilize a Shopify app that costs a monthly fee.

In early 2013, Shopify rolled out Shopify Payments, its own, native credit card payment-processing gateway as an alternative offering to the already established payment gateways. To entice Shopify storeowners to use their payment system, Shopify waives all transaction feeds normally applied to all transactions. Normally, you pay an extra 1-2% transaction fee to Shopify on every transaction made through your website, when using a third-party payment processor.

Shopify removes such fees when you opt to enlist Shopify Payments as your processer. Normal credit card processing fees still remain when using Shopify's payment processing system and the percentage ranges based on which account plan you utilize. Although Shopify makes money off storeowners using their processing gateway, you will ultimately save money using their processing, plus your customers will enjoy a more seamless checkout experience because everything is handled by Shopify.

The credit card processing fees charged by Shopify when using Shopify Payments are very competitive with other credit card processing companies, so most storeowners should enlist their Shopify Payments. However, if you already operate a high volume retail operation and have a great processing system in place, you may wish to neglect using Shopify Payments – especially if their rates can beat those charged by Shopify Payments.

In terms of paying for your Shopify account, you must connect a Visa, Mastercard or American Express card to your account to pay for the monthly subscription cost of running your store. You will be billed every 30 days automatically and will be notified/invoiced every time this occurs for your convenience.

Shopify currently offers four account levels, of which the majority of features mentioned in the last chapters can be found across all account levels, leaving only several advanced features like the abandoned cart functionality and gift card creator for those subscribing to the higher priced plans.

Below you will find the current account options at the time of this book's publication.

It is also advised to look over Shopify's account offerings yourself to see if any changes to price or features have occurred.

Starter Plan

The first plan is the $14/month "Starter Plan". There is a transaction fee of 2% of your sales with this account; again, this is waived if you use Shopify Payments for your payment processing. The Shopify Payments' processing fees for this account include a 2.9% charge, plus $.30 flat processing fee, and a 2.7% charge for in-person transactions.

All of the basics are covered with this plan, including the ability to list 25 products and 1 GB of storage. You can use any theme from the Shopify theme store, but cannot modify it. And that's it. It's exactly what it says it is, a starter plan, and this is recommended for those new to online selling or those with just a few products ready to go. A few of my smaller clients are running highly efficient online stores and bringing in sales using just the "Starter Plan".

Basic Plan

The next plan is the $29/month "Basic Plan". There is a transaction fee of 2%, which is again waived if you use Shopify Payments for your payment processing. The Shopify Payments' processing fees for this account include a 2.9%, plus $.30 flat fee processing fee, and a 2.7% charge for in-person transactions.

As for additional features, you get unlimited products, 1 GB of storage and access to Shopify's discount code engine, which allows you to offer discounts to your customers.

Professional Plan

Next up is the "Professional Plan" which is currently offered at $79/month. Credit card transaction fees are 2.5%, plus the $.30 flat processing fee, with a 2.4% charge for in-person transactions. The transaction fee is reduced to 1% with this plan, which again is waived when you enlist Shopify Payments.

Additional benefits include 5 GB of file storage, unlimited products, discount code engine, gift card processing, generated reports, and abandoned shopping cart support - a feature which employs a number of tools to increase revenue by helping you target those visitors to your site who have abandoned their order online. Many eCommerce experts have found that abandoned carts account for a 60% to 80% loss of sales across the board annually.

In my opinion, this plan is the best account offered by Shopify or any online store builder for that matter. The abandoned cart feature, which we will discuss later on, is worth more than $79/month by itself. This plan gives you access to the most important features, lower processing fees, and the ability to really build a complete eCommerce experience for your customers – all for under $100/month. This is quite an incredible feat for the eCommerce industry as a whole, considering any individual can create a word class online store for less than the cost of their cable bill.

Unlimited Plan

The "Unlimited Plan" is offered at $179/month. Credit card transaction rates are 2.25% plus $.30 per online transaction, with in-person credit card transactions coming at a rate of 2.15% with no additional fee.

The Unlimited plan gives you all the features that were just mentioned, as well as an advanced report builder, a more involved version of the Professional plan's report generator which allows you to export results and filter data. This can be invaluable to serious storeowners and larger businesses with persons in place to analyze these reports.

The Unlimited plan also offers real time shipping information. By partnering with UPS, FedEx and the US Postal Service, Shopify will calculate shipping rates based on real time pricing rates, which allows your store to accurately charge shipping fees to customers in real time based on their location.

Annual, prepaid plans are also available for the four plans mentioned above, which will give you a 10% discount on the annual cost of the plan for one-year plans and a 20% discount for a two-year prepaid plan. Obviously, you need enough money up-front to cover the cost of these plans, so for those that do, and are confident they'll want to stay with Shopify, it's a good deal.

For those more hesitant to commit, or are trying out a new business, the monthly plan is for you.

Plus Plan

Shopify also offers a "Plus Plan", usually advertised to retailers expecting over $1 million in sales. This is a custom plan, and you have to contact Shopify for details.

This will hopefully give you a good idea of which account will best meet your needs. I would recommend the "Basic" or "Professional Plan" to those ready to get their store up and running. You will have access to everything needed to operate a fully functional, customizable store at a great price.

Now armed with a solid understanding of Shopify's capabilities and the account necessary for you to run your business, let's dive into getting your online store up and running.

Setting Up Your Account

Setting up an account with Shopify is easy.

To get started, fire up your browser and head to http://www.3stepwebsites.com/shopify-trial.

There is a free, 14-day trial for getting your store up and running; you should utilize this promotion because you can explore Shopify without having to pay a cent. You will be able to test the various features and make sure you will have everything you need for your store. Once ready, you can activate one of the accounts just mentioned that fits your needs; you will then begin paying the account's respective monthly rate.

To start, you must enter in a name for your store. You can change your name later, but the name you choose here does create your "myshopify" store URL (www.johnsstore.myshopify.com), which can't be changed, so this is an important decision. Multiple-word names will create a hyphenated URL (like your-personal-store.myshopify.com).

Regardless, most merchants will go on to link their own domain to the store or simply buy a domain from Shopify. If you have your own domain, you will be able to change your URL from the "myshopify" URL to your own URL later on.

Enter your store name, your e-mail address, and a password, and click the button that says "Try Shopify Free" to start. You'll be taken to a screen where you'll enter some basic information, such as your name, phone number, address, and what kinds of things you'll be selling in your store.

Shopify will then take you to your "Dashboard," a content management system (CMS), which you'll use to set up and manage your store. This is the "backend" of your site. What the user sees in their browser when they navigate to your site is the "front end" where they can navigate all of your products.

Shopify's CMS is similar to Wordpress and other popular site-building platforms; this makes it easy for people who have never built or managed a website to do so with their very clear and concise navigational layout.

Once inside of your Dashboard, you will see a list of tasks to get your site up and running. Let's take a look.

Account Settings

Your account settings screen is where you can control and alter the basic details of your account. You can access this screen by going to "settings" on your administrator panel, then clicking "Account," at the bottom of the left panel. Here, you'll see all the basic details of your Shopify account.

At the top of the page, you'll see your plan type and details. This shows you the plan in which you are currently enrolled, plus some information about what that plan entails. You can upgrade your plan at any time by clicking "Change plan type," on the left side of the page.

Under "account overview," you can see your credit card details, as they are registered with Shopify. If you have not yet set up a credit card as your primary payment source for funding your Shopify account, now is a great time to do so. Click "add a credit card," and then enter your credit card details at the following screen. You can also choose "change credit card," if you'd like to replace the one you currently have on file with a different card.

In the "staff members" section you can add staff members to your Shopify store. This is very helpful if you have more than one employee and would like each employee to have access to your Shopify account. As the account owner, you have ultimate control of your store and will be able to delegate extremely pinpointed access to your staff. With each new staff member, you can select from a variety of checkboxes the areas of your store they can control, such as adding new products or adding content to the blog.

Beneath that, you can view invoices for your monthly Shopify payments, and change the email address where you'd like to receive your invoices.

Finally, if you decide to delegate responsibility of your store to someone else or want to register it under another username, you can do so in the "change account owner," category. This is different than adding a "staff member" as you will be delegating complete control to a new person or party.

Getting to Know Your Shopify Dashboard

After you log in to your account, which you can always do from this URL, https://www.shopify.com/login, you will enter your Shop's Dashboard.

Aside from being the starting place for accessing all areas of your store's backend, the Dashboard provides a quick look at your Shopify account's recent activity and provides you with some important statistical metrics that will help you assess the popularity, visibility, and frequency of activity of your Shopify business.

Familiarizing yourself with the dashboard display will help you to glean a quick snapshot of how your Shopfiy business is faring. The dashboard is meant to provide you with a clear and brief encapsulation of recent activity on your account. Note that, when you first set up your Shopify account, many of these statistics will not be present, and some of the options described below will not yet be available. These numbers will compile as you use your Shopify account more to sell your products and will soon become visible.

The top bar will provide you with the total sales, in dollars, and number of orders for the specified time period. You will see that each statistical box in the top row gives you the option of viewing different sales periods: today, yesterday, the last 7 days, last 30 days, or last 90 days.

To toggle among these screens, simply click on the box for the time period you would like to view. Note, too, that you can select different dates by clicking in the date box, in the top right-hand corner of your dashboard screen, and input the date you'd like to view from the dropdown menu.

Once you have selected your desired date or date range, you will be presented with a number of statistical categories. Understanding and monitoring these categories will help you track the progress of you store.

Beneath the graphic showing your total dollar amount earned in the specified date range, you will see another number indicating the number of orders. This refers to the number of total checkouts, not total items, which your Shopify account has processed within that date range. The dollar amount indicates the total value of these transactions.

Visitors

Beneath these graphics, on the left side of your dashboard screen, you will see your visitors information log. This area of your dashboard offers information on people who have visited your Shopify account, and the means by which they arrived there. Visitors are grouped into a few categories:

Direct visitors are those who navigated straight to your Shopify site, by directly accessing its URL. This means, essentially, that the visitor either typed your Shopify page's address into his browser, or clicked a direct link within an email or other kind of personal message.

Referrals are visitors who arrived at your site by clicking a link on another website. This could have been a link that was embedded in advertising, or a link shared on social media such as Facebook, Twitter, or Pinterest

Search Engine visits are from those users who used a search engine, such as Google or Bing, to search terms that provided them with a link to your Shopify site. These search terms may have been explicitly intended to search for your Shopify site, or they may have merely closely mirrored the content which is available on your Shopify site, prompting the search engine to the direct the user to your Shopify page.

Traffic Source

Visitors will be broken down into one of the above categories and presented in the "Traffic Source" section of your dashboard. These numbers will be presented both as absolute figures, and as a percentage of your total visits. This is a great way to gauge where your Shopify traffic is coming from, in the service of honing your advertising and outreach methods.

To get more insight into incoming traffic, click on the "View Stats" option. Here, you will see several graphical representations of incoming traffic, including pie charts and a bar graph. If you scroll down on the page, you will see statistics on social media referrals and search engine visits, on the left hand side.

The social media referrals section shows incoming traffic from sites like Facebook, Twitter, and Pinterest, and which site accounts for which percentage of total social media referrals. The search engine number show similar statistics, but for particular the various search engines. Beneath this, you will also see information on your visitors' countries of origin. This can be useful especially if you are trying to reach an international audience or make inroads in foreign markets.

Top Referrals

Back on the main dashboard screen, next to your Traffic Source pane, you will also see a list of Top Referrals. These are the top three sites that direct the most traffic to your Shopify page. Monitoring your top referrals is a good way of figuring out which third-party sites have been the most effective at bringing your Shopify page to the attention of potential customers.

You will also see a "top search terms" category, showing the terms that visitors have typed into search engines, which ultimately brought them to your store. You can also click the "view report" option here to see graphical representations of your top referrals, and to filter referrals by different payment and order options.

This is incredibly important information to storeowners because you can see what ultimately leads to sales. One of your tweets may have brought a ton of visitors to your store, but no sales; where an email may have prompted only a few visits, but the majority of visitors made a purchase. This is where Shopify truly over delivers and gives you a complete selling platform.

Total Sales

The total sales tab will show sales and purchase data for the time period selected. You can get information on your product sales, which products are selling the most, and see how often browsing customers actually become paying ones.

Beneath the total sales heading, you will see a graph of your sales for that period. Note that the time scale will change depending on your selected time period. So, if you are examining sales figures on a daily basis, you will see hourly sales statistics, whereas sales across the month will be shown day-by-day.

Website Conversions

Next to your total sales graph, you will see your website conversions information. The website conversions pane gives you valuable information about your shoppers' browsing and buying experiences on your Shopify page. When a customer adds an item to her cart, she will then be prompted to either continue shopping, or proceed to checkout. At the checkout stage, the customer will enter shipping and payment information. Finally, the customer will be prompted to complete her purchase.

Shopify logs how far each customer makes it in the purchase process. Ideally, 100% of shoppers who add items to their carts will complete purchases, although this is rarely the case. However, these statistics can be very useful for seeing if there is a particular stage in your checkout process that is hanging up a lot of customers and preventing purchases. Shopify offers some options that can help enhance the shopping experience at various stages, and these may help improve your conversion percentage.

Note that statistics are compiled based on how far *each individual* shopper got on your page. So, if someone added an item to a cart, proceeded to checkout, but then did not complete a purchase, that visitor would only be logged once, in the "reached checkout" category.

Top Sellers

The top sellers pane showcases your three highest-selling products. It will show a thumbnail of the product, along with a number of total sales. This is a quick way of checking on your most popular items. Within the "view report" window, you can see your top seller graph, and also filter by categories like individual items, vendors, and product types.

Activity Feed

If you scroll down your dashboard, you will see the activity feed section. The activity feed is essentially a running log of all your Shopify account activity. Data included on your activity feed can run the gamut from product updates and additions, to technical adjustments or access grants.

To see activity pertaining only to action taking place on the account itself, but not within your Shopify store, select **"account activity,"** in the upper right-hand corner of the activity feed. If you'd prefer to only see transactions taking place on your store, and hide administrative account activity, select **"store activity."** To see everything happening on your Shopify account and within your Shopify store, select **"all activity."**

Building Your Shopify Store

Designing Your Store

The design of your online store is more important than ever; it's your digital storefront, so the look and feel of it should represent your business, and most importantly, help guide visitors seamlessly around your store and incite visitors to take specific action (join your email list, purchase a product, view the most recent sale).

Shopify provides a wide selection of store designs to choose from, referred to as themes. There are both free and premium themes to select from; additionally, any theme can be modified to meet your exact design needs.

Shopify allows third-party, professional web designers to create themes to sell to storeowners, providing you even more theme options to select from. Shopify has it's own theme store with 100+ themes, both free and paid, but you can find amazing Shopify themes for download or sale around the web.

A quick Google search for Shopify themes and storefront designers will return turns of themes to browser through, or simply head over to a theme marketplace where many of third-party designers have their themes listed for sale or download. Popular theme marketplaces include www.themeforest.net and www.shopifythemes.net.

Ideally, themes found in Shopify's theme store will be best since you are guaranteed support/updates directly from Shopify. However, most professional web designers offer support and updates as well, and in some instances, will deliver an even better theme solution for storeowners.

Either way, you should avoid creating or paying a designer to build you a custom theme because Shopify themes are known for their incredibly effective eCommerce themes. Save yourself the headache and the money of building a custom theme; rather, just spend more time researching and selecting any of the already available themes that will meet your business's needs.

Choosing a Theme

Shopify maintains a theme store, much like iTunes, Google Play, or any other marketplace that offers digital goods. Here you can select a free or paid theme, all of which are designed and tested by Shopify-contracted designers before being added to the theme marketplace. There are sortable filters on a left-hand sidebar, so that you can select from a range of prices, or sort store themes by industry. You don't have to choose a theme based on these industries - these are simply suggestions.

Different eCommerce web stores have different needs. For instance, if you're selling photographs or clothing garments, you may prefer a more "curated" feel for your shop. These needs may be best matched with a theme that displays large, high-quality photos prominently throughout the theme.

If you're a larger retailer with tons of varying products, you will most likely prefer functionality and organization that can help users navigate through your various product categories and sub-categories.

Pro-Tip
Before browsing and selecting from the various themes, write down of all of your store's functionality needs and desired appearance. This will help you narrow your theme search, and also prevent you from selecting a theme that has a lot of glitz and glamor, but doesn't provide what you need.

Once you have this list of needed capabilities, you can reference the Shopify's theme selection guide to help you meet you match your business needs with a theme.

You can find the guide here: http://docs.shopify.com/support/your-website/themes/choosing-a-theme/

Free Vs. Premium Theme

Shopify currently offers around 100 themes to select from. Some are free, while others range in price from $80-$180.

Unlike most online store platforms, the free themes provided by Shopify should meet the needs of the majority of storeowners. Again, just cross-reference your list of required capabilities with the available free themes to see if they will work for you.

Premium themes can offer more features and functionality than the free themes, and some can be visually more appealing. All premium themes purchased on Shopify carry just a one-time cost (no recurring fees), making purchasing a theme a very reasonable option for most business owners considering these themes come with a price tag of less than $200.

I would advise utilizing a free theme during your Free Trial period, that way you can focus on getting comfortable with your dashboard, adding products to your store, and making sure the essential pieces like payment processing and taking orders are in place. Once you've got everything set up, you can then decide if a different theme will better match your store's needs. You can change themes at anytime, and can have 8 themes uploaded to your admin dashboard, so switching between themes is really easy.

It's important to note that most themes contain various styles to choose from as well. Not only do you have your say in which theme to use for your store, but also, most themes have various color schemes and layouts that you can further select from. These different layouts can be viewed from within the Shopify Theme Store where you can look at examples of the theme being used in the varying ways.

When browsing the store, select a desired theme and scroll to the bottom of the theme's page and you will find a section with the different styles you can select from if you use that theme.

Responsive Themes

As discussed earlier, online stores must take into account the increasing amount of traffic coming from mobile devices, and this is where responsive design comes into play.

Many of the Shopify themes utilize a "responsive design". This means that your store will adjust its layout to fit the screen of the device viewing it. Everything from your store's navigational layout to the sizing of images and buttons will change in size and placement, yet all functionalities remain intact. Responsive design guarantees that every visitor will be presented with the optimal layout for their device, which increases both your customers' viewing and shopping experience.

Shopify has utilized responsive design in building many of their themes, with the majority of these themes being premium. Selecting a responsive theme for your store is certainly my first recommendation for the majority of storeowners, but other themes may better suit your store's needs.

Regular / Desktop Themes

Aside from selecting a responsive theme for your store, you can select a regularly designed **desktop theme**, so that regardless of the device being used by your visitor, your online store will appear the same.

So instead of your store's theme "responding" to the device viewing it, it will remain static and all viewers will see the same layout.

The upsides for using just one theme are that you won't have to worry about having a mobile website in place and visitors will always have the same experience when visiting your website.

The downside of not having a responsive design or a mobile website in place is that mobile visitors may have to zoom in or scroll more to navigate your website.

If you are using a regular theme and want to ensure it appears similarly for all of your visitors, you should double check that your settings are correct. Your theme will need to be set as both your desktop and mobile theme. From your theme manager, you can set any theme to be your mobile theme. In the "Themes" section, just click "Publish" and then "Publish as mobile". This should be done automatically for you, but always worth checking to make sure it's set properly if your shop isn't working properly on mobile devices.

Desktop themes may be better for some businesses that have massive stores, with many moving parts. You may have a certain agenda for your visitors; responsive themes can sometimes resize and move parts of your store around that may through this agenda off.

Mobile Themes

Your last option, instead of using just a desktop theme or a responsive theme, is to have two themes working simultaneously, both a desktop theme and mobile theme. This means that visitors using their computers will see your store's desktop theme and those visiting your website from their mobile device will see your mobile theme.

The upside for having two themes is that you can adjust/enhance your visitors' experience because the better-suited theme will be shown to them automatically based on their device.

The downside is that you will now have to manage two themes and make certain decisions twice (once for each theme). There really isn't too much more work involved with going this route, but it may cause enough confusion for novice storeowners that it's not worth doing.

Pro Tip
Using a single theme, regardless of whether it is responsive or not, is recommended for most storeowners. Having both a regular and a mobile theme is a somewhat outdated way of catering to your mobile visitors and is not highly recommended.

My strong recommendation would be to just select a "responsive" theme so all visitors feel as if they are receiving a tailored shopping experience. Plus, this makes for less administrative tasks and you can spend more time on the important areas of your business.

Previewing Themes

To get a better idea of what a theme will actually look like in your store, you can preview a theme. You can do this by clicking on a theme in the Theme Store, and selecting the left-hand green button that says "Preview Theme in your Store."

This will give you temporary access to the theme, which will run from your backend dashboard. You will get to see a live preview of your store using the theme, but won't be able to activate it until you've purchased the theme (or in the case of a free theme, downloaded it).

If you go back into your administrative dashboard, and select "Themes," you'll see the theme you're previewing in the "Theme Preview" section. Here, you can see the preview by clicking "preview," next to the theme's name, modify the theme settings by clicking "Theme Settings," buy the theme (if it's premium), by clicking "Purchase," or delete the theme by clicking the trash can icon.

Downloading a Theme from the Theme Store

When you find the theme you'd like to use for your eCommerce store, click "Get Theme" on that theme's page. Free themes will be denoted by "FREE" above this button. Premium themes will state the price above this button.

If it's a premium theme, you'll see a window that says "Approve Charge," which will give the theme's name and price. You'll have two options. You can approve the charge, which will be billed to the credit card associated with your site, or you can decline. Hit the "Approve charge" button to buy the theme, or hit "Decline" to go back to the previous screen.

When you approve payment, you'll have a couple different options on how to proceed. A page will appear saying that you're about to install the theme on the account you are logged into (make sure you're logged into your correct store if you have more than one). You can click "Publish as my shop's theme," which will immediately install the theme and publish it, thus un-publishing your shop's current theme.

Or you can click the options below: "download theme as .zip," to download your theme onto your computer, or "install as an unpublished theme". I'd suggest installing the theme as an unpublished theme; that way it gets placed in your dashboard to be activated after you've reviewed the new layout and you've determined if the new theme will demand new content, images, etc.

Regardless of install option, your theme can now be edited from the "Themes" section of your dashboard.

If you downloaded the file, you'll have to manually upload it to this theme area.

You can also buy a theme that you've previewed in your backend by going to "Theme Preview" on your "Theme" page in the admin and clicking on "Purchase."

Paid themes from Shopify's theme marketplace are currently non-refundable so review that your theme meets your store's needs before purchasing.

You can store up to 8 themes in your dashboard/backend. If you attempt to add more than 8 themes, you will be denied until you remove or export a theme.

Uploading a Theme

If you bought a theme outside of the Shopify theme store, or downloaded your theme from the Shopify theme store, you will need to upload it to your store before you can use it.

Your theme should have been downloaded as a compressed .zip file, a common file extension, in order for you to successfully upload into your Shopify dashboard.

To upload your theme, go to the "Themes" section of your admin. Click the top-right button in the "Themes" header that says, "Upload a Theme." A dialog box labeled "Upload a Theme" pops up. Click "Choose File," and select your theme's file from where it's stored on your computer, select it, and click "Upload". Your theme will now be available in the "Themes" page of the admin, under "Unpublished Themes."

Adding Products to Your Store

There are several ways for adding products to your store; you can enter them manually, import them from a previous store, or upload them from a CSV spreadsheet file.

When adding new products to your online store, make sure to save your product listing as you go just in case you navigate away from the page or there is an Internet connection error. The product pages we will now discuss have "Save" and "Save and Close" buttons for just this reason.

Let's first look at the various settings and options you have when manually adding products to your online store.

Manually Entering Products

For most storeowners with a small inventory of products and/or constantly testing different products, manually entering products will be the best choice for adding new products to your store.

To begin entering products, go to the "Products" area of your Shopify dashboard. Next, click the "Add a Product" button in the upper right-hand corner of the page and a product information window will now appear.

There are a couple different fields in this window: "Title" and "Description," which are text fields, and "Type" and "Vendor," which are drop-down menus.

Title and Description

"Title" is the title of your product. This will be your product's name in your store.

Your title should be simple and descriptive; the product's brand, what type of product it is, and any keywords that are crucial to visitors finding your product.

"Description" is the product's description, the written copy that your customers will see when they view your products. The "Description" field has a mini-text editor, allowing you to use bold, italics, bullet points, and other options, including embedding images or video.

Your description should also include the main keywords that visitors may be using to find this product. You can use Google's Keyword Planner to identify the best keywords to use and to see which keywords are searched most by your potential customers.

In addition to including keywords, your description should satisfy nearly every question a customer might have that is associated with their need. It's also important to pay attention to the style of your description; first, avoid typos and grammatical errors, and secondly, use a voice in your description that is appropriate for your brand.

Give customers an idea of why they'd want your product, its benefits or what problems it solves, and do this succinctly. Also, it's a good idea to order the information about your product from most- to least-important, and hit those marks within your copy.

Product descriptions are immensely important. If you don't answer the customer's questions, or your product description copy sounds unprofessional, you will lose sales. Check out what some of the major brands do with their product descriptions and also take note of what your competitors are doing for their best selling items.

Type and Vendor

"Type" means the type of product this is. This field is mandatory.

The drop-down offers a broad product range. Select the one that most closely matches your product.

"Vendor" means the manufacturer or supplier of the product. Enter this information in the "Vendor" field.

Inventory, Price, and Other Options

There are a number of fields in the "Inventory and Variants" section on the "Add a Product" page. When you navigate to "Inventory and Variants," you'll see a field for "Price," "Compare at Price," "SKU," and "Barcode," as well as check boxes for "Charge Taxes" and "Require a Shipping Address," a field for "Weight," and a drop-down for whether you want Shopify to track your inventory:

Price and Compare at Price

"Price" is simply your product's price. When entering a price, you should not enter a currency symbol. Just type a number with a decimal to indicate your price. If needed, your store's currency can be adjusted in general settings.

"Compare at Price" is where you can insert the price of the product as most commonly seen across other stores. Certainly use this component if you offer a competitively priced product, as this will help convert browsing visitors to paying customers. This price will be displayed with a strike-through when appearing on your store, indicating that your price is better than that of the average retailer also offering the product.

SKU

You should always enter a SKU (stock-keeping unit) number for your products. Assigning SKUs helps you stay organized, identify your products, and properly fulfill orders. For products with different variants, you must give each variant its own SKU. Product variants can include sizing, color, etc. We will discuss variants further in an upcoming section.

Ensuring there's a unique SKU for every variant of your product is important. When Shopify records a sale, this unique SKU will be included to the order making it easier for the person fulfilling the order (you or another party) to correctly identify and ship the correct item(s).

For instance, your baseball hat may come in three colors; thus, the black hat, red hat, and green hat will all have their own SKU for uniquely identifying the right colored hat.

Shopify does not generate SKUs for you automatically; you must create them yourself. SKUs are arbitrary numbers, so they can be anything, but you should create some type of system for easily creating and identifying SKUs. For example, all of your products that are hats can be assigned an SKU that starts with "1".

Pro Tip
Make a simple spreadsheet to keep track of your entire inventory and add a column for SKUs so you can quickly reference all of your products. If needed, you can provide this spreadsheet to your fulfillment center/warehouse to help save them time and you money.

Barcode

If there's a barcode on your product, type it in the "Barcode" field. If your product doesn't have a barcode, or you don't plan to have a physical point of sale, you may leave this field blank.

Charge Taxes and Weight

Check this box if you are charging taxes for this product. Tax and shipping options are handled at a different location in your Shopify admin, which we will fully address.

Require a Shipping Address and Weight

If you're selling a physical good (and not a digital product), check the box for "Require a Shipping Address." When you do, a field for "Weight" will appear below. Like your price, you can only enter in a figure, and not a unit of measure. Your weight options can be selected in your "General Settings".

Note: When entering in a weight, include the weight of your packaging.

The "Weight" option is important if you intend to use third-party fulfillment, as it helps calculate shipping fees. Shopify rounds up weight to the nearest gram, so enter in as exact a weight as you can.

Owning a basic digital scale can be helpful at this point, although manufacturers should supply this information to you. You can use manufacturer-supplied weight to approximate, but it's a good idea to double-check for deviations. If you are using a fulfillment service to complete your orders, you absolutely want to enter in as exact a weight as you can, that way you can correctly calculate your shipping costs which will dictate if and how you charge your customers for shipping.

Fulfillment

The fulfillment section is where you can select who will be fulfilling orders of this product. Since Shopify provides you the functionality to partner with third-party fulfillment providers, such as Amazon's fulfillment service (Fulfillment By Amazon), here is where you will have the option to select your fulfillment provider.

You must have already added your fulfillment provider into the fulfillment area of your dashboard already (we will go over how to do this) in order to see a drop-down menu where you can select your provider. If you haven't selected a third-party fulfillment option, you won't see this drop-down menu.

Inventory Policy

Shopify can keep track of inventory on your behalf which may sound pretty basic, but actually is quite a powerful function for storeowners. If you want Shopify to track inventory of your product, select "Shopify tracks this product's delivery" from the drop-down menu. When you do, a field marked "Quantity" will appear next to the drop-down menu. Enter in the quantity of your product here.

We'll get to inventory management when we talk about running your store; this will help prevent you from selling items that you do not have in stock.

Options and Variants

Below the options we've already talked about, there will be a check box that reads: "This product has multiple options."

You are provided with a wide range of options and variants, and these options and variants are product-specific. Each item can display a range of variants that shoppers can choose from.

For instance, an article of clothing that comes in a variety of colors or sizes can display each of those variants as a separate choice for the customer, while, in the backend, you can quickly and easily set them and edit them all at once.

The Difference Between Options and Variants

If you have a store selling hats, you will create your product listing called "hat". Within this listing, you will now want to clarify the different sizes and colors that this hat comes in.

To do this, you must first create the **product's options**, of which you are limited to a maximum of three options. These options should be used to explain what the differences of your products are, for example the "size" of the hat and the "color" of the hat.

With your options created, you must now describe how each of these differences changes the product the customer is purchasing. For example, you can assign several values to the color option, which would include the values red and blue. Within your "size" option, you can add the values: small, medium, and large.

Now, when you save your product's listing, your **products variants** will be established. Using our example, you will have created a total of 6 variants of your product:

Hat: small, red
Hat: small, blue
Hat: medium, red
Hat: medium, blue
Hat: large, red
Hat: large, blue

Setting Options and Variants

Shopify allows up to 3 option categories per product. To add options, check the box in your product information window that says, "This product has multiple options," located beneath the fields for "Price," "SKU," and others.

In the "Option Name" field, select an option (size, color, etc.) in the drop-down menu, for which you wish to add. By default Shopify includes options, but if you don't see an option you need, you can create one.

Next, enter the values this option provides into the field that says "Option Values," directly next to the "Option Name" field. Option values have to be separated by a comma. Once you enter these option values, they will appear as buttons you can delete by clicking the "x" next to each variant in the "Option Values" field.

Once you save your work, you will be shown the variants created in a list form. Each variant will be listed in a left-hand column with a range of editing and organizing options. Make sure your options and variants are accurate (and that you don't, for instance, offer colors in one size that you don't offer in others). If you need to edit and organize, you can do very easily; so don't get caught up in the confusing terminology here. Just create your options, add values, and then check to see if the variants created match up correctly with your inventory.

Creating a Product Option

Creating a new product option is simple. Navigate to your product info and find the option called "Inventory and variants." Click on "edit options" and then select the button that says "Add another option". Then, enter in a new category option and hit Save.

Your new option will be available in the "Option Name" drop-down menu in the product info section.

Bulk Actions

Shopify gives you a way to save time when entering in options and variants. Let's say you just added a new hat color to your inventory and want to make sure all new variants are created. Select the "color" option from the top of the list in "Inventory and

Variants," and click the "Bulk actions" button below.

Now, under "Duplicate Variants" in the drop-down menu, click the product option you want to enter values for. A box will pop up allowing you to type in a new value. Click "Done" when you're finished, and the new variants will be generated, taking into account this new color option.

You can also edit or delete options and variants in bulk actions, as well, or edit an individual one by clicking on it in the "Inventory and variants" section.

Product Images

The "Images" area allows you to add images of your product to your listing. The "Images" section can be found from within the "Add Product" section.

In the "Images" section, you can upload files of your products, which will be included alongside your product description. Click "Choose Files," and a window will appear. Select your product images by pressing "Open," (because this is your local operating system such as Windows or Mac, the exact text on the button will may differ).

Images will now be displayed in a list. You can drag and drop the image you wish to be the most prominently featured image of your product to the top. This will make it the "featured" image. The "featured" image is the primary image that will be displayed next to your product, and users will have an option to cycle through the other images you upload.

Optimizing Your Images

You ideally want images that if resized, do no distort. To ensure that your images appear in proportion at any size and do not distort, they must share the same "aspect ratio". The aspect ratio is the ratio of the width of the image compared to height. Image dimensions are usually expressed in pixels, abbreviated as px. A 200px by 200px image has an aspect ratio of 1:1 and a 200px by 400px image has an aspect ratio of 1:2.

If you were to take a 400px by 800px image and resize it down to 200px by 400px, it would have the same aspect ratio, 1:2. This is important, because many parts of your layout in your Shopify store theme will display images, and then resize images to fit elsewhere on your site or resize to better fit on mobile devices. If your images have divergent aspect ratios, your images will look bad, and this could have a negative impact on your sales.

You should also pay attention to image resolution, frequently expressed as "dpi," dots per inch. There are no set rules for image resolution requirements, but higher dpi means a sharper image, while a lower dpi means images are more pixelated, or blurry when viewed on a monitor.

If you resize a lower-resolution image to larger dimensions, the results are very blurry. If you size down a high dpi image, the image will remain clearly defined. Having images with higher dpi also means a larger file size, so this may be something worth considering if you have a lot of images throughout your store as data storage is factored in to your Shopify account's monthly pricing.

Manufacturers will usually supply images when you buy their products, but if these are unsatisfactory, you should take your own.

Lastly, it's usually recommended to have your main product's photo contain a white background as to only display the product in a clear fashion. You do not want to include accessories in the photo or a snapshot of the product being used as to confuse visitors as to what exactly they will be purchasing. Certainly add action photos and photos of only those accessories included as your additional photos.

Product Tags

Tags are identifying keywords relating to your product. Tagging your products provides you an additional way to help your customers navigate your store and find what they're looking for. The best way to use tags is to simply use keywords that describe your product. You can add more than one tag to a product.

For example, you may "tag" your hat's listing with the tags "hat", "accessory", and "headwear". Customers will then see these tags appear on the product listing with the option to click on any tag. Clicking the tag "hat" will bring up a page with all of your products that you have tagged "hat", helping them narrow their search to show only your products that they are interested in.

Tagging your products is also a great way to increase your product page's SEO value. Search engines will begin to show your page with all products tagged "hat" in their search results for when users type in "hat". Thus, tagging your products is one of the most effective, yet simple-to-execute SEO tactics.

To enter tags, go to the "Add product" section and click on a particular product. There you'll find a section labeled "Tags". Enter tags by typing each one into the field provided, separated by a comma. Delete them by clicking the "x" next to a tag's name. You'll also be prompted with previously used tags that you can add to your listing. To add a tag to a product, just click on the tag to select it.

There is no way to edit tags in a bulk action. However, once a particular tag is no longer used for any of your products, it will no longer appear as a tag in your dashboard. Before assigning tags to your products, do some light research on which keywords make the most sense for tagging purposes.

Pro Tip
Browse Amazon and Google products listings for keyword suggestions to use for your tags. Imitate those listings with the most reviews and that appear to come up first in your different searches. This is a surefire way to ensure you select the best keywords for your products that will help customers find your product and also help the search engines accurately display your products for the keywords/tags you decide to use.

Search Engines

For many storeowners, search engines provide the majority of visiting traffic to their store, so let's look at the "Search Engines" section of your product pages.

The "Search Engines" section lets you submit three important pieces of information for each of your product listings: the title, the meta description, and the product page's specific URL.

Shopify automatically generates these three pieces of information, using the product description and title you have already entered to display on the page.

It is very important to note that the title and description you've crafted for your product's page are different than the title and meta description you submit to search engines. Many online storeowners never realize that there is a difference between the two; not understanding this difference can be quite costly to one's business.

Shopify has realized the confusion that this has caused many storeowners, which is why they've created this search engine section. It allows you to enter in a unique title and description for the sole purpose of providing information to the search engines.

Search engines use this information in two ways. First, they analyze this information to identify what your website's page is about. This will help your page/product appear in search engines' results from the most pertinent queries.

For example, Google will analyze your product's listing and determine that it's a "blue baseball hat" and whenever someone searches for a "blue baseball hat," Google will display your product's page somewhere in it's list of results. Thus, the more accurate information you provide to Google, the higher your product's page will appear in search results.

The second use search engines have for this information is for display purposes. The title, description, and URL that you enter in the "Search Engines" section displays in the search engines' results. See the image below to see how the information you enter appears in Google's search results.

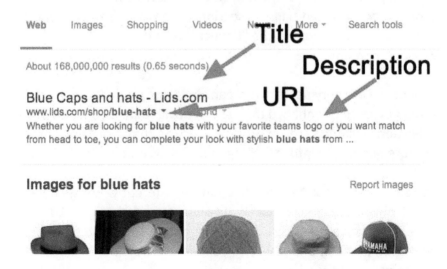

The last Search Engine criteria you control in this section is the URL to be used for your product's page. You will simply want to use the same keywords you've decided on for your title, description, and tags for your URL. Hyphens should be used to separate keywords that are phrases like in the example above, "blue-hats". This phrase will be appended to the end of your URL, giving search engines even more data for evaluating your page.

Entering these three information pieces is easy - just enter your data into the corresponding fields. Enter your title where it says "Page title," description where it says "Meta description," and URL phrase where it says "URL & Handle" fields.

Collections

"Collections" are products you choose to group together for both your own organizational purposes, and to enhance your customers' experience. "Collections" are found in your "Add a Product" pages, giving you the option to add your product to a collection. You can click on "Add to Collections" to bring up a drop-down menu of collections you've created.

If this is your first product, you won't have any collections to choose from. You can skip this section since you can add products to collections from within the "Collections" section in your dashboard at any time.

Collections are very useful for organizing your products and should be used to enhance the ease of navigation. Good uses of collections include types of products such as "hats" or "sneakers" or more general/helpful groupings such as "Women's" or "Kids".

You should also look to use collections in different ways, such as by price. You can create collections of items priced under $10 or have a clearance collection. Another common collection type can be seasonal collections where all your "back to school" products can be grouped together.

Visibility

Shopify gives you the ability to keep your product from appearing in your store. This gives you the ability to work on your products listings and save the work you've done without having to publish it live to your site.

Head to the "Visibility" section from within the product's pages and you will find two sets of check boxes: "On your website" and "On Shopify POS." If you haven't installed the Shopify POS app, disregard this one. If you want your product to be visible, check the box next to "Visible". Checking the "Hidden" box will keep your product from appearing in your store until you decide it's ready to go.

You can also set a publishing date/time for your products. This will be important to those storeowners looking to setup certain times for launching sales, etc.

From within the "Visibility" section, click "Set a specific publish date..." below "On your website," to set your publishing date.

Importing Products in Bulk

If you already have an eCommerce store, you may be looking for a quick way to migrate your entire inventory to Shopify at once. Shopify luckily offers such as a feature, which will save you tons of time. Even if you do not already have a store, you can still utilize this method if you have a ton of inventory you would like to add as products in your store.

To import products, navigate to the "Products" section of your Shopify admin. If you've never added or imported products, you'll see two buttons: "Add a product" and "Import products." If you've already manually added products, the option to import products will be in the top menu bar of the "Products" page, as a button reading "Import," to the right of the "Export" button.

You'll now have the ability to import from a CSV (a file which can be read and edited in a spreadsheet program such as Microsft Excel), or from other eCommerce platforms, which you can do by clicking the link that says "Need to import products from another platform?".

When you click the link, you'll see a list of eCommerce services Shopify can import products from. If your service is on the list, you'll be directed to download the Shopify Importer app specific to that service. The steps for importing from other eCommerce services are unique to each service. Shopify walks you through the simple process for each of the stores, making it as simple as possible for you to leave your old store behind!

If you don't see the service you wish to import from, you can click the "Cancel" button, and import from a CSV.

Importing From a CSV

CSV stands for "comma-separated values." It's a plain text format where data is ordered by line breaks and separated by a character, usually a comma. Using a CSV file to import products is an extremely efficient way to provide product information in a standard measure, which by uploading to Shopify, gets interpreted and added to you store in a way that is compatible with their platform.

The "Import Products By CSV" option is available from the "Products" section if you've already added or imported products, or from the "Add a product" section of your backend, in which you'll click "Import products." If you have added or imported products, clicking "Import" in the top menu bar of the "Products" page will bring up the "Import Products by CSV" option.

To import your CSV data, it must match the format of this Shopify template (http://docs.shopify.com/manual/your-store/products/product_template.csv).

You can also create a CSV from scratch in a spreadsheet program such as Microsoft Excel, Open Office, or Libre Office, following the template provided by Shopify. It is absolutely crucial that you follow their instructions so that your product information is imported correctly.

In the "Import Products By CSV" section, click the "Choose File" button, and navigate the local file window that pops up. The window will allow you to choose a file from your computer. Click the "Open" button to choose your file. Now click the "Upload file" button.

If your upload was successful, you'll receive a conformation file that will be sent to the email address associated with your account. If not, Shopify has a troubleshooter, which you can find here (http://docs.shopify.com/manual/your-store/6-products/8-common-import-issues).

Once you've finished, you can modify your inventory using the methods we detailed above. Image files, for instance, cannot be contained within a CSV, so you'll have to manually add them yourself, or, if you're importing images hosted on another site, you can add the links to your images in a column of your CSV.

It's important to note that you can't import gift cards via this method. In fact, if you try to, your next import attempt will fail. This is because every eCommerce platform hosts gift card information differently. You will need to manually enter these.

Pro Tips
For those storeowners selling digital products, you will have to use an app in order to sell and handle orders of digital products. The best Shopify app is called FetchApp, and this makes it incredibly easy for adding digital products to your store and delivering these products to customers once they've placed their orders.

For those storeowners selling services, it's suggested (not required) to use an app to make it easier to sell your services. I would recommend using the BookThatApp for adding real-time booking functionalities to your services. You may also want to consider the Product Options app that allows you to add more information about your services, more than a regular product description allows for.

The pages section of your dashboard is designed to facilitate the creation of web pages for your Shopify site. Having more web pages makes for a more immersive experience for shoppers, and so the creation of a couple of well-designed web pages is strongly encouraged.

To access the main Pages screen, select "pages" from the left navigation pane from any page within the Shopify administrator account. At the main Pages screen, you will see a list of your current webpages. Shopify provides you with two readymade pages: a "Welcome" page, which is the equivalent of your shop's landing, or front, page, and an "About Us" section, where you can fill in information about your Shopify shop.

From this screen, you can also search pages, using the search box at the top of the screen, and filter pages. Now, we'll take a closer look at editing and creating new pages.

Editing Existing Pages

As mentioned above, Shopify has already created two pages for your convenience: a Welcome page and an About Us page. Since these are standard templates, you will likely want to create your own, personalized versions of each of these pages. Editing web pages on Shopify is fast, easy, and intuitive.

To do so, click on the name of the page you'd like to edit, from the main Pages screen. You will then be redirected to the editing screen. In the top "title" box, you can rename the page by deleting any existing text and typing in your new page title. This is the title customers will see when they are navigating through your Shopify site, so it is important to make sure the title of the page is clear and tells visitors very directly what kind of content they can expect to find on that page.

Beneath the "title" box, you will see the "content" box. This is where you can place the text you'd like to appear on your web page. Clear the existing text in the box, and begin composing your web content. Note that the rows of icons represent formatting and content options. Formatting-wise you can change the font style, alignment and indent settings, and text color.

On the right hand side of this icon row, you will see options to insert hyperlinks (links to other websites), tables, images, and video. Adding these items to your web page makes for a better browsing experience, and increases the likelihood that any visitor will become immersed in that page's content.

Once you have finished adding text, links, and media to your web page, you can view the page, as it will appear to your visitors, by clicking on "Preview page," in the upper right-hand corner. If all looks well, click "Save," also in the upper right-hand corner, and your page will be added to your Shopify site.

Adding New Pages

To add a new page, click "Add page," in the upper right-hand corner of your main Pages screen. On the page creation screen, you will see both "content" and "title" boxes, whose functions and capabilities are described above, in "Editing Existing Pages." Beneath the "content" box, you will also see a "search engine" pane. Similar to product listings, you can use the boxes labeled "page title" and "meta description" to manage how your web page will be conveyed to the search engines.

Beneath these boxes, you will see "URL & Handle." Here, you can set the web address for your newly created Shopify page. Try to create a URL that is as descriptive as possible of the content on your page. (For example, you might want to name your page full of information about winter hats "http://YOURSITE.myshopify.com/pages/winter-hats".)

The last option, at the bottom of the page, controls the page's visibility. Most pages you create should be marked as "Visible," so that all potential customers visiting your site can see the page. However, if you are developing a page, or would like to create one that is only intended to be seen by staff and administrators with access to your Shopify account, you may want to create a "Hidden" page.

When you are done creating your page content, you can again select "save," in the upper right-hand corner.

Blogging with Shopify

Like the Pages section, the Blogging section of your dashboard enables you to quickly create blog posts for your Shopify site. Just as with webpages, blog posts help garner interest from potential customers, and give you a more informal and real time outlet for sharing news and content with your visitors.

Before getting into the specifics of blogging on Shopify, it's important to first delineate the difference between pages and blogs. While the creation and maintenance of both is a similar process, they do have distinct differences, and it's important to keep these in mind when deciding whether to create a new page or blog post. Generally speaking, pages are permanent fixtures on your site. You may update, move, or entirely delete a webpage from time to time, but these are pages that are unlikely to change very often.

Pages are ideal for describing your Shopify store, company history, listing contact information, or adding content that rarely changes or becomes outdated. Conversely, blog posts are meant to reflect current trends and events happening in your industry or specific to your business.

You might want to use a blog post to highlight a recent industry trend, a company milestone, or a newly released product in your store. You should add new content to your blog with some regularity, while pages do not necessarily need to ever be changed. Search engines favor stores that regularly add content to their site, especially blog posts, with the assumption that your store is being curated, kept up-to-date, and is delivering great value to the visitors it sends your way.

To access the main blogging screen, click "Blog Posts" on the left navigation toolbar from within your Shopify administrator account. At the main blog screen, you will see a list of your existing blog posts. Shopify automatically provides you with one blog post, "First Post," so that you can get started blogging right away. Once you begin to add your own blog posts, you will see them accumulate in a list on this screen.

Creating Blog Posts

You can begin blogging either by clicking on the readymade "First Post," which is primed for editing, or by clicking "Add blog post," in the upper right-hand corner of your screen. The process is the same in either case. Once you have arrived at the blog creation screen, type your new blog post's title in the "Title" box.

Blog titles should be direct, short, and easy to understand, so that your potential customers will understand what the post is about without having to even read the content of the post. After titling your post, add the blog content in the "Content" box below the title box. As with webpages, you can adjust the font and format of your post in many ways, and insert media, from photos to videos.

Once you have completed your blog post, select an author and a blog from the dropdown listing beneath the content box. If you have multiple individuals managing your Shopify site, select the name of the author of the blog post. Then, select the blog you'd like the post to appear on. Most Shopify stores maintain just one blog, the "News" default, but if you have multiple discrete audiences, you may want to create a number of different blogs to cater to specific audiences.

You'll notice that, above the "author" dropdown, is the option to add an excerpt. Adding an excerpt is a good way to draw attention to your blog. Excerpts can be photos or a few lines from your blog posting that will appear to customers visiting your Shopify main blog page. Adding excerpts to blogs can increase their visibility and make it more likely that customers will visit your Shopify blog.

As with pages, you will also have the option to add tags describing your blog post, search engine terms, and control the visibility of the blog post. Once you have entered this information, click "Save" in the top right hand corner, and your new blog post will be created.

Managing Blog Comments

Whenever you maintain a blog on any website, there is the ability to allow visitors to comment on your blog posts. This can create a great community atmosphere and encourage others to visit your blog and Shopify store.

However, there are some risks associated with allowing an open forum to take place on your website, including the possibility of negative or obscene posts appearing on your site. Learning to manage and control commenting on your blog posts is a critical part of maintaining your Shopify blog.

To manage the commenting settings for your blog or blogs, click "Manage blogs," at the top of your main blogs screen. About a third down the page, you will see a comments section with three options. Select the option that seems best for your blog format:

Comments are disabled: Users are unable to post comments on any blogs on your website.

Comments are allowed, pending moderation: Users are able to post comments on your blog, but these comments will not be published until you have approved the comment. This is a good way to control exactly what appears on your site, but entails a good amount of extra work for you.

Comments are allowed, and are automatically published: Users are able to post comments, and these will be published directly to your blog, without any preapproval from you. This is an easy way to allow comments on your blog, but will also allow any comment to appear on your blog. Remember that you can always delete an individual blog comment if you find it objectionable.

Once you have selected the appropriate option, click "save" in the upper right-hand corner to save those settings for the blog.

Navigation refers to the way that visiting customers will interact with your Shopify store, specifically, how they will move from page to page, and how links within your store are organized. By default, Shopify organizes links for you, but it's important to understand how to manually manage your store's navigation settings.

You can access your navigation menu from the left pane within the administrator view. Once on the navigation page, you will see your "link lists," lists showing the navigation options that will be presented to visitors to your Shopify page. Shopify has already supplied you with two navigational lists, main menu and footer. The main menu will appear at the top of your page, while the footer appears at the bottom (in most cases, depending on theme).

Editing Link Lists

To personalize your page, you can add links and rearrange the order of links within individual link lists. It is useful to conduct these processes while keeping an eye on your actual Shopify store page, refreshing periodically to see if the changes have dictated the desired effect.

To begin personalizing your link lists, click "edit link list," beneath the list you would like to edit. At the top of the page, you will see a box where you can edit the name of the link list, if you so choose. Beneath that, you will see your actual link list, as it currently exists.

Link lists are divided into a few columns: the leftmost, "link name" shows the text that visitors to your store will see on your Shopify page. You can click in this box and edit link name text if you want.

The next column, "Links To..." dictates which section of your store the link name will redirect to. Since a link name can only redirect to an existing part of your site, you must select a site section from the dropdown menu. The first seven options are internal, meaning they will redirect within Shopify, will the eighth option, "Web Address," can be used to redirect users to external webpages.

After you have selected the link category from the dropdown menu, another column will appear, if applicable. Here, you will be asked to select the sub-page you would like the link name to redirect to.

For example, if you selected "Pages" in the previous column, but have created multiple web pages, at this step you will be asked to select the *specific* web page you'd like visitors to be directed to. If you selected "Web Address" in the previous step, you will be presented with a box where you can type the URL of the website you'd like to redirect to.

Once you have established your link list and link paths, Shopify offers you some further editing opportunities.

First, you can change the order in which links will appear on your link list. To do so, click on the icon of the two very small rows of dots, to the left of the "link name" column. Your mouse icon will turn into a cross cursor and you can click and drag the link name to the desired position. Your link list will then appear in the order you determine. If you'd like to delete a link at any point, simply click the trash bin icon, to the extreme right of the link, and the link will be deleted from your list.

To add another link to your link list, click "Add another link," to the left of the link columns. The new link will appear at the bottom of your link list.

After you are done modifying your link list, click "save." Back on the main navigation page, you can add further link lists, if you desire. Depending on your theme, there may be more locations for adding link lists, such as a sidebar navigational menu or a dropdown menu. You will want to create a new list for these areas.

Click "Add link list," on the left side of the page. Give your link list a new name, and then assemble it the same way you would modify an existing link list.

Creating Product Collections

You can create collections by clicking the "Collections" section in your dashboard. Click "Add collection" and then enter in a name and short description for your collection. Assuming you've already added a few products, you will now click "manually select products" and press save.

Now, you can scroll down to "Products". Here you can search for your products that you would like to add to the collection, adding as many products as you want by clicking on the name. Press Save when you are done adding all desired products to the collection.

You can utilize the Smart Collection function to have products automatically added to collections. This process should only be used for storeowners with hundreds of products; otherwise it's not worth the time it takes to create. If you do have such inventory, click here to learn how to setup a smart collection.

Shopify Store Settings

From within your dashboard, the settings menu is where you will adjust your Shopify store's settings. The settings menu controls essential information to keep your store operating correctly, so it's important to understand the options available to you from within settings.

General Store Settings

Your general settings tab gives you the ability to input and adjust some basic information about your Shopify account and Shopify store. Access your settings via the left navigation bar from your main administrator screen. When you open settings, it will automatically navigate to the general tab. You will notice other settings menus are available in the left navigation pane. Some of these tabs are covered below.

Store Details

In the first section of general settings, "store details," you can set and change your store name. This is the name of your Shopify store that visitors will see on your Shopify page. If you would like to change your store name, simply change the text in the "store name" box, and then click "save," in the upper right-hand corner.

You can also enter information for your homepage title and your homepage meta description. Both of these data points will be used for search engine purposes, and will aid your search engine optimization, that is, the ability for potential customers to find your Shopify store via a regular web search. The homepage title can describe the basic content of your store, while the meta description should be a clear, concise paragraph describing the products your store offers.

Beneath these two boxes, you will see your account's email and customer email settings. The account email is the address Shopify will use to contact *you*, while the customer email is the email address that will appear to customers when you email them through Shopify. You can change these addresses if you want, and then click "save," to ensure that the changes go into effect.

Store Address

The store address is the physical address of your company or store. If you have incorporated your business, or otherwise legally codified its existence, you can put the business's legal name in the top box, "Legal Name of Business." If your business has a physical address, you can add it here; if not, add your home or alternate office address.

Standards & Formats

The standards and formats section relates to units and data tracking mechanisms on your Shopify store.

Order ID: Shopify defaults to starting all orders with 1001, but you can append numbers to the front of the order, by adding a digit between "#" and the "{{number}}" text, if you would like to.

Time Zone: Select your local time zone. Shopify has helpful regional data for those unsure of their local time zone.

Unit system: Select either imperial, for the United States and territories, or metric, for rest of world measurements. Note that these are the units your customers will see as well, so it may be useful to consider your primary customers at this stage.

Currency: Shopify will default to the local currency specified by the information given in your payment account. You cannot change your currency from this screen, only from within the Checkout and Payment section.

Google Analytics

Google Analytics is a website analytics platform that will help you track and analyze visits to your website. In the settings menu, all you need to do is copy and paste your Google Analytics code into the text box.

For a further discussion and instruction on setting up an analytics account with Google, please visit here - http://docs.shopify.com/manual/settings/general/google-analytics

The majority of sales analytics and reporting is handled thoroughly by Shopify and you will have more than enough information to understand how your store is operating. Google Analytics will better help you track the traffic coming to your site, what pages they frequent most, and more in-depth analytics to help you find opportunities within your business.

It is recommended that you utilize Google Analytics, and at the very least, install the tracking code so data can be collected for future use. It only takes a few minutes to set up, and once set up, there's no ongoing work on your end. The data will be collected on autopilot, allowing you to visit and revisit the data at anytime in the future.

Storefront Password

It is possible to password protect your Shopify store by entering a storefront password. Note that password protecting your Shopify store will prevent it from appearing in search engine results and visitors will need to enter the password to access your store. This is clearly not recommended.

To add password protection, click the "password protect your storefront," box, and then enter your password. You will also have the option of entering a message for visitors to the site, explaining your password protected situation, if you like. Click "save," and the changes will go into effect.

Note, too, that if you have not yet launched your Shopify store by providing credit card information, and enabling the site to go live, your store will be automatically password protected by a password generated by Shopify. This will disappear once your site has gone live.

Setting Your Shipping & Tax Rates

If you're selling physical goods, Shopify provides some generic shipping rates on your behalf, which you adjust at any time. If you would like to adjust taxes associated with transactions, you can do that as well.

You can also indicate that you've included taxes and shipping into your item's pricing to better inform your customer. As much as these are administrative tasks, they affect your products' pricing, which ultimately affects your marketing efforts, so be wary of all costs and prices associated with both taxes and shipping.

With varying state tax rates and constant updating of online retail legislation, we won't get into too much detail here. It's up to you (U.S. storeowners) to do your own research and comply with one's own state's tax regulations.

Shipping Rates

Shopify offers two basic modes of setting up your shipping rates: manual setting your rates and carrier-calculated setting of your rates. Also, a third setting, when using a fulfillment service, will appear.

General shipping settings can be found by going to "settings," from with the dashboard, and then by selecting "shipping." Before selecting your shipping method, you should input your shipping address, by clicking "Add one now," at the top of the page. This is the address from where you'll be shipping goods.

After you add your shipping address, you will see rate-setting categories for each of your three shipping options: shipping rates for manual shipping, carrier-calculated shipping, and Fulfillment/Drop shipping.

If you are going to send your products manually from your home or office address and do the necessary shipping work yourself, you should only use the "shipping rates" category.

If you are going to use UPS, FedEx or other national carriers and want your shipping costs to reflect their real-time rates, enable "carrier-calculated shipping".

If you select manual shipping, you should also input the countries where you intend to ship your goods to. Shopify will automatically add your country of residence and a blanket "rest of world" category. These calculations are somewhat arbitrary and preliminary, and so you should adjust these as necessary if you plan on shipping to countries other than your own.

This can be done by clicking "Add shipping rate," and inputting the specific shipping rate you'd like to add. If you find yourself shipping to a specific international country very often, you can always add that country at any time, by clicking "Add a country," and input specific shipping costs, aside from your "rest of world" costs.

Shopify offers you incredibly detailed control over your shipping costs and settings. While the above instruction will suffice for most storeowners, a complete shipping guide can be found here, http://docs.shopify.com/manual/settings/shipping, on Shopify's website.

Setting Tax Rates

Shopify provides thorough tax settings for storeowners. Unless you have a very textured appreciation of shipping and sales tax and would like to set those taxes manually, we strongly advise allowing Shopify to manually calculate tax. Navigate to your settings panel from your administrator dashboard, and then click "Taxes." Here, you'll see the countries for which taxes are already set up.

As before, Shopify will automatically add tax data for your country of origin. You can see more advanced tax data by clicking on any country and exploring the pop-out. To make sure taxes are being automatically calculated, ensure that "I want to specify taxes automatically" is checked in the pop-out box.

Below the "tax rates" settings, you will see a "tax settings" box. Here, you can decide whether or not to display prices in your store with tax *already* added. Customers may appreciate the transparency of this gesture, but it might also muddy your pricing scheme and display unappealing prices (for example, a product that was listed at $9.99 with a 4% sales tax would appear in your store at $10.38, or so). In these settings, you also have the option to add taxes to your shipping rates.

The last thing to be aware of within the taxes menu is the possibility of setting up a tax override. Before doing so, you must be aware of whether or not particular products that you sell are eligible for state tax exemptions. If you have been selling the product for some time and are already aware that it is tax exempt for some reason, you can click "add tax override."

Select the region for which the tax exemption applies, and then specify the product. It is often a good idea to have products grouped into collections, as these tax exemptions usually apply to whole ranges of goods. Select the collection of products, and then manually adjust the tax rate. Click "add override" when you are done.

Setting Up Payment Processing

Choosing a payment processing solution is a very important decision for every retailr. Retailers must select a company to handle all of their credit card transactions in order to comply with banking and security regulations.

Shopify has recently created their own payment processing solution, Shopify Payments, to offer a more integrated processing solution for storeowners using their platform.

They also have partnerships with 70+ third-party payment processors, such as Paypal, so the option is up to you for enlisting a processing company.

When selecting a processing solution that best meets your business's needs, it is important to assess the varying costs and transactional fees, as well as how each payment processor integrates into the checkout process.

Shopify Payments

Shopify Payments will be the best option for the majority of storeowners due to the incredibly easy integration process, allowing you to see both your sales and inventory data alongside revenue and payment information. If using a third-party solution, you will have to look at both sales data and payment data separately.

Additionally, enlisting Shopify Payments as your payment gateway has its perks. Not only will you be instantly approved and ready to take orders, you will also avoid the 1-2% transaction fees (this is the normal fee Shopify charges with every sale made through your store when not using their payment processor). You will also be able to process returns and payments from your Shopify dashboard, saving you time and headache that usually comes with managing both your sales channel and payment processing.

Shopify Payments is set as the default payment processor for new accounts in North America. It is currently only offered to storeowners in the United States and Canada. It's visible in the "Set up Payments" panel in the administrator dashboard when you first sign up. Click the link telling you to "Configure Checkout and Payment Settings," and click the green "Complete Shopify Payments account setup" button, where you'll be taken to a short questionnaire, which is used to determine the nature of your business, primarily what type of products you're selling and what your typical sales are.

You can also fill in information as to what your customer will see in their credit statement, and fill in information on what checking account your revenue will be deposited in. Submit the form by clicking the green "Complete account setup" button.

Third-Party Payment Gateways

You can also integrate your Shopify store with any of the major third-party payment gateways such as Paypal, Stripe, Authorize.net, and more. Selecting one of these third-party companies may provide more competitive rates depending on the volume of sales your store produces.

Overall, Shopify Payments will most likely be the best solution for almost every merchant because you will avoid the 1-2% transaction fees applied to all of your sales. It will be very difficult to find a third-party processing company that will be able offer a better processing rate when you take into account the transaction fees you will be also paying.

Operating Your Store

With your store designed, and basic settings accounted for, let's look at some of the more operational elements and how to best maintain an efficient online store.

In this section, you'll learn a little about some of the regular activities you'll perform to keep your Shopify store running and profitable, as well as some advanced operations such as making discount codes to attract new customers.

Before going live with your store, you will want to double check that you've completed the essential steps outlined in this book. Here's a quick checklist of what to review before going live:

- Check Tax & Shipping Settings
- Check Your Store's Domain Status
- Conduct a Test Purchase
- Launch Your Store!

Check Tax & Shipping Settings

First, head to your products page and click on one of your products. Within your product listing, scroll down to "inventory and variants" and click "edit". Here is where you can check to see that "charge taxes" and "require a shipping address" are checked, assuming you need to include these for your products (exceptions could be stores with digital goods). Lastly, check to see that you enter the weight of product into the appropriate field as well.

Check Your Store's Domain Status

First, head to the "Domains" section with Settings of your dashboard. Check to see that your domain's status does not say "needs more configuration – get more info". If it does, click the link and follow the directions for completing setup of your domain. If all set, it should just show a checkmark with the word "OK" underneath the status for your domain. Make sure you set the domain you wish to be your store's domain as the primary domain. The domain being used as your store's primary domain will say "Yes" underneath the Primary Domain column.

Conduct a Test Purchase

Once you have your store settings aligned and payment processor activated, you'll want to make a test purchase to ensure your store is in working order. You definitely want to do this, because if there's a technical hiccup in the purchasing process, not only will you lose money, your early-adopting customers, a vitally important group to nurture, will conclude that your store doesn't work.

You can conduct a test purchase using one of two ways.

Use a Bogus Gateway

Shopify makes it easy to test your store without having to actually conduct a transaction. They created a fake payment gateway that you can activate for testing. Everything except the transaction will be tested to see if working properly: orders, shipping, inventory, taxes, etc.

Head to the checkout section in your dashboard and deactivate your current payment gateway. Now, from within the top section, choose "Select a Credit Card Gateway" from the Accept Payments dropdown; select "Bogus Gateway" and activate it.

You can now go to your store and place orders. When you need to input a credit card number, enter a 1, 2, or 3 to simulate different results: 1 will enact a successful transaction, 2 will enact a failed transaction, and 3 will simulate an exception such as a payment gateway error.

And that's it. You can check your store's backend to see that it went through (if you simulated a successful transaction).

Real Payment Gateway

The other option is to simply test a real order, and then just cancel the order.

First, check to make sure your real payment gateway is activated; then, make a real purchase from your storefront. Next, in your backend, cancel the order to refund your purchase and avoid any transaction fees. Do this right after you place the order to avoid fees.

Launch Your Store

Within your Store's general settings, find the "Storefront Password" section and uncheck the "Password protect your storefront" box. Save changes and your store will now be live, without needing a password to see any of the pages or products.

Shopify is great at capturing orders, managing your orders, and helping facilitate returns. Let's explore the main steps involved during the order process.

After an Order is Placed

As soon as an order is placed through your Shopify store, you will be notified via email. You will also notice, upon logging into your Shopify account, that there is a badge next to the Orders tab, indicating the number of new orders. To view your new orders, simply click on the "orders" tab on the left navigation pane. You will then be taken to your main orders page, where you will see a list of all orders and their payment statuses.

It's important to note here that, in order to have payment from orders captured, meaning that you receive money from your customers, you have to have *already* set up a payment method, via the accept payments settings. For more information on this process, see the preceding section, "Setting Up Payment Processing." These settings will dictate how you ultimately will receive payment.

Once you payment has been made for an order, you can now fulfill the order. Every person and business will have their own fulfillment process, but there are certain useful settings in regards to fulfillment.

Automatic order fulfillment will automatically ship your goods once payment has been received on an individual order. Automatic fulfillment is great if you are selling digital goods that can be delivered right away, or if you utilize a third-party fulfillment service that keeps stock of your goods and processes shipping orders for you.

To activate this option, go to your Settings tab, in the left administrative pane, then, select "Checkout," from that screen's left pane directory. Scroll down to the "order processing" section and select "Automatically fulfill the order's line items," beneath "After an order has been paid." Now, every order will be fulfilled automatically after payment is received.

Manual order fulfillment is the more common setting for most storeowners. You will fulfill the customer's order; Shopify will not take any automatic action. To activate this option, return to the Checkout section within the Settings tab, and scroll back to "order processing." Select "Do not automatically fulfill any of the order's line items," beneath "after an order has been paid."

If you choose to manually fulfill orders, you will have to take additional steps to fulfill orders coming into your store. To do so, go to the Orders page on your administrator panel. Then, select the order you would like to fulfill, by clicking on it. Unfulfilled orders will show that they are "not fulfilled," in your main orders page.

Once you have selected the order, click the "fulfill" button in the upper left-hand corner. Shopify will automatically show you the items to be fulfilled, based on the order. You will also have an option at this stage to check a box to "send a notification email to the customer," alerting the customer that the order has been fulfilled. You can also attach a tracking number at this stage, if you'd like.

Then, click the "fulfill items" box at the bottom of the page. A green truck icon will appear next to the items in the order, and you will now see your recently fulfilled order under your Order History, at the bottom of the page.

Canceling or Refunding an Order

You may want to cancel an order that has been placed, or refund an order that has already been shipped.

To cancel an order, go to your Orders main page. Click on the order you need to cancel, and then click "cancel order," in the upper right-hand corner. You will then be presented with a cancel order dialogue. Select the reason for canceling the order, and then choose whether or not you'd like to restock the items. If you expect to get the items back, or have not yet sent them out, you should restock them so that your Shopify inventory will reflect the current number of products.

You can also choose whether or not to send a notification email to your customer that the order has been canceled. Click "cancel order" at the bottom of the page, and the order will be cancelled.

To refund an order, click on the order you would like to refund. Then, click on the "Refund" button at the top of the page. Enter the number of items you need to refund. If you need to refund the whole order, simply enter the same number that appears in the "ordered" column in the "refund" column. If you want to refund individual items, only enter a number in the refund column for those items. Shopify will present you with the total to be refunded, minus the cost of shipping. To also refund shipping, simply enter the cost of shipping, also shown on this page.

Once you have your refund information established, choose whether or not to send a notification email, and then click the button that says "Refund," plus the dollar amount, at the bottom of the page.

Customer Management

Just as your orders page tracks exist orders that come into your Shopify store, the customers page tracks customers who've ordered from your store. Keeping track of customers is a great way to not only streamline your order fulfillment process, but to also gather information on your customer's spending and buying habits.

To look at your customer list, click "Customers," from the administrative navigation pane. Here, you will see a list of all your existing customers, that is, individuals who have placed orders with your Shopify store. From this screen, you can view any customer's information by clicking on the customer name. You can also search for specific customers by name by using the search box at the top of the page. Shopify also allows you to filter your customers page by specific criteria, such as money spent, number of orders placed, and date of last order.

This is especially useful if you are trying to target a specific portion of your customer base for a marketing campaign or similar promotional activity. To filter your customer list, click "Filter customers," in the left corner near the top of the page, then select your filter category. Input the detail required, if necessary, and then click "Add filter." Shopify will display only customers who fulfill the filter requirements.

Adding, Importing and Editing Customers

You can add new names to your customer list from the main customer administrator page. Click "Add a customer," in the top right-hand corner. Fill out the form on the subsequent page with as much data as possible, including the customer's name, contact information and physical address. You can also add notes about the customer, if you'd like, or add tags.

Adding tags can provide you with the option to filter quickly later by searching for specific tags, and can also help you group customers into target groups for marketing purposes.

Once you are done filling in your new customer information, click "save," in the bottom right-hand corner.

You will then be taken to that customer's main information page. Note that, in the top right-hand corner, there are two buttons, one trash icon and one edit button. If you would like to completely delete the customer account, you can click the trash icon. To edit the customer's information instead, click the "edit" button. You can update and refine the customer's contact and personal information.

If you have a preexisting list of customers, and would like to batch import it into Shopify, you can do so using the import function. To do so, you must first create a CSV (comma separated value) document, as this is the only format that Shopify will accept for your customer import list. If you have already been tracking your customers in a program like Microsoft Excel, you need only to save your document in that program as a CSV (comma-separated value) file (usually found in File>Save As). You can also use a plain-text program, such as Notepad for Windows or TextEdit for Mac.

Once you have created your CSV file, you can import it by going to the main Customers administrative page and selected "import," in the upper right-hand corner. You will then be asked to locate the CSV file on your computer. Once you have selected this file, your customer information will be uploaded to your customer page.

You can edit individual entries by the process described above. Note that you can also export your current customers as a CSV file, if you would like to keep your customer list in Excel or a similar program. Click the "export" button, also in the top right-hand corner. Your customer list will then be sent to your email as a CSV file.

Creating Discounts

Creating discounts is a great way to attract new customers and reward loyal customers. Codes for discounts can be distributed via social media and other platforms, enticing potential new customers to visit your store.

There are two general types of discounts that can be produced: dollar-based and percentage-based discounts. While dollar-based discounts offer a finite dollar amount of savings (e.g., $25), percentage-based discounts offer a percentage (e.g. 10%) off the total final sale.

You should consider the merits of each, relative to the goods your Shopify store provides, and then follow the instructions below to set up your preferred kind of discount. Shopify also provides other discount options, such as free shipping to further incentivize shopping at your store.

To set up a discount, go to the Discounts page, found on your main administrative tool pane. In the upper right-hand corner, click on the option to "add a discount". Under "discount details," enter your discount code. This is the code customers will have to provide to be able to redeem the discount with your Shopify store. You can enter a creative discount code if you like (e.g., FREESHOES), or simply click "Generate code," on the left-hand side, and Shopify will assign a random discount code.

Beneath the discount code box, determine whether or not you would like to set a limit on the number of times the discount can be used. Click the "No limit" checkbox to make the discount infinitely redeemable, or unclick it and set the number of times the discount can be redeemed in the box to the left. (Remember that you can always disable and delete discounts, rendering them irredeemable for everyone.)

Beneath the discount details, you will find the "Discount type" criteria, where you can set your discount type and amount. To set a dollar amount, select "$ USD" from the dropdown menu, and then type the dollar amount you would like to discount into the box to the right. In the dropdown menu, further right, you can specify if you'd like to discount all orders, orders over a specific dollar value, or for specific customers, products, or groups of products. (Note that, if you are using another currency, you will see that currency amount, instead of USD in the leftmost box.)

If you'd prefer to set a percentage amount, select "% Discount" from the leftmost dropdown menu, then enter the percentage amount in the box to the right. You can enter the same stipulations about when you would like the percentage discount to apply, as with the dollar discount.

In the last option row, "Date range," you have the ability to specify your discount start and stop dates. This is good for "limited time only" discounts and the like. Click in the start date box to select a discount start date from the calendar pop-up. Do the same for the discount end date to set a finite discount range. If you prefer to extend the discount indefinitely, click the "Never expires" checkbox, all the way to the right.

Once you have set your discount details, click "Save," in the upper or lower right-hand corner. You will then return to the main discounts page, where you will see the discounts you have created.

If you would like to stop the discounts at any time, for whatever reason, you have two options: you can either disable or delete the discount. To disable the discount, click the "Disable" button, on the main Discounts page, to the right of the discount you'd like to disable. If you disable a discount, you can reactivate the same discount at any time by clicking the same button, which will read "Enable."

Doing so will reinstate the discount under the original terms. If you would like to do away with the discount completely, you can click the trashcan icon to the right of the discount, deleting it. Note that, once you delete a discount, it is gone from the system forever and cannot be reactivated.

Adding Gift Cards to Your Store

You can allow customers to purchase gift cards from your store, just as they would purchase any other product. Customers can use the gift card until the balance runs out, using it all towards one purchase or split among separate purchases.

To activate selling gift cards on your store, head to the "Gift Card" page and click "Start selling gift cards on my store". You will need to have at least the "Professional Plan" activated as your account level to use the gift card feature.

By default, your first gift card will be created and a product listing will be created, but the gift card will not be made available for sale. The product listing for your gift card will include 4 variants – priced at $10, $25, $50, and at $100.

To activate and edit this gift card listing, head to your products as it is listed among all of your products. Since by default it is not activated, you will have to mark it as visible so it appears for sale. You can then change any of the variants (which is the just dollar amount of cards offered), adding new denominations or deleting the default denominations.

Customers can purchase your gift cards, just as they would normally purchase a product, the only difference being that they are sent an email notification containing a URL so they can view their gift card. Here, they can view, print, or email the gift card, and also start shopping by navigating back to your store.

Additional gift card information and functionalities can be found in the Gift Card section of your dashboard, including how to issue a new gift card for promotional purposes, manage all outstanding gift cards, and customizing the notification email that purchasers of gift cards receive. You can even create a separate product collection for your gift cards as to better organize their placement in your storefront.

Shopify Reports

In order to make it easier to view your store's progress, Shopify provides you with a Reports area, where you can track sales, orders, and payments. You can access the reporting area via your administrator panel, under "reports."

Reports are grouped into four different categories: products (relating to items sold in your store), orders (relating to customer orders made to your store), payments (relating to payment you have received from customers), and taxes (which provides valuable information on your tax responsibilities for profits earned via your Shopify store).

From your main Reports screen, you can click on any subcategory within the four main categories described above to view a particular report. Report data is presented as a bar graph and, below that, as a data table. Hovering your mouse over particular areas of either the bar graph or the table will sometimes give you additional information about a particular data point.

There are a few features that can help you get a more granular snapshot of your reports data, regardless of the kind of report you are viewing. Note that there is a report range, at the top of each individual reports page, which allows you to specify the date range you'd like to see on that data screen.

You can access your report range by clicking the down arrow icon and using the calendar pop-out. You can select specific dates, or see preset date ranges, such as the past seven or past thirty days. Within a table, you can also "zoom-in" on a data point by clicking the grey arrow icon, where available, next to a statistical category.

For example, if you would like to see sales numbers by state, within the United States, you can click on the arrow icon, next to

United States sales, and see state-by-state data. Note that this feature is only available for some data points.

Just as with your customers and orders data, reports data can also be exported as a CSV file. Just click the ellipsis symbol (…) at the top of the page, then select "Export." Shopify will email you a CSV file of the data on the current screen, which you can open in programs like Microsoft Excel.

Notifications

The notifications section of your administrative backend is where you can edit emails that are automatically sent when routine action takes place on your Shopify store. There are many email templates that are automatically created by Shopify for different scenarios, and personalizing and specifying when they are sent helps put a more personal touch on your store's outreach presence.

There are a variety of email notifications for which you can use and customize to your liking. These emails are automatically sent out, either to you or the customer, depending on the type of notification. For example, customers will receive an order confirmation email, which you can customize here or leave the default settings.

You can access the notifications section by navigating to your settings menu, from your main administrator panel, and then selecting "notifications," on the settings administrator panel.

On this screen, you will see all the existing email templates. Shopify has created a template email for each situation that is likely to require one, and so you should not have to create any new email templates.

You can, however, edit the existing templates if you like. To do so, click on the template you'd like to edit. You'll be redirected to the text-editing window, where you can change the existing text to reflect a more personalized message. Note that email templates are written in a mix of HTML (a computer programming language) and plain text, and that performing edits to the HTML without proper HTML knowledge will likely render the email templates useless.

Luckily, Shopify provides you with a guide to the HTML terms used in template emails so you can better understand the template text you are viewing. This guide is available back on the main notifications screen, linked from the bottom of the explanatory paragraph on the left-hand side ("See also the templates variables documentation.").

Once you have finished editing your email template, you can click "Preview," on the bottom of the text-edit window to view a preview of your email. You can also send a test email to your own email account to ensure that it displays properly.

Once you are satisfied with the changes you've made, click "save," in the text edit window. Your new template will now be automatically sent.

Helpful Shopify Resources

Since Shopify is essentially an online community of small business owners, it is crucial that Shopify storeowners have continual access to troubleshooting and other help resources.

Shopify is extremely aware of this need, and as such, has produced and provided a wealth of materials that will help you address any issues that may arise, and also aid you in enhancing your store.

All of the resources listed below can be found at here http://docs.shopify.com on the page or in the footer links.

Shopify Docs is a compendium of basic lessons that, as an assemblage, essentially function as a Shopify manual. These docs cover the basics of everything from setting up and running your store to advanced troubleshooting and store-building techniques. The Shopify Docs are usually a reliable first stop for quick technical fixes and the like, and can also provide you with more insight into processes or functions you are already using on Shopify, revealing new features that you were not already aware of.

ECommerce Forums are places where Shopify users and experts can get together to discuss all varieties of Shopify issues. Discussions are grouped into different subcategories covering everything from accounting and tax questions to feedback on individual stores.

It's important to remember that the forums are comprised of fellow Shopify users, with the occasional Shopify expert chiming in. This may not provide the most reliable source of all your Shopify information, but other forum members will certainly provide in-depth insight into various aspects of the Shopify experience.

Shopify Experts are for-hire Shopify experts who will perform a wide range of Shopify activities for you, all designed to help expand your store's professional appeal and online reach.

While using this service necessitates budgeting some extra funds to pay your Shopify Expert, the expertise you gain can often be quite useful. If you feel like stuck or just want to ensure the best shopping experience for your customer, it's probably worth taking a look at what some of these services for-hire.

ECommerce University is Shopify's native instruction page, offering a vast base of Shopify knowledge and instruction upon which you can build the foundation for a very productive Shopify business. Getting through all the information presented in the ECommerce University presents a significant time commitment, so it may be better to begin with a targeted approach to the materials, rather than attempting to go through all of it at once.

The best place to start is with the ECommerce *free guides*, short instructional guides, available for free, and offered in a wide range of topics. Choose one that is likely to cover the information most useful to you at your particular stage in the Shopify process. These guides will help you better understand various aspects of running your Shopify business and, hopefully, increase your sales.

When you've got the handle of running your store, check out some of the *case studies*, so that you can get a better idea of real-world examples of successful Shopify stores and find concepts that could also be applied to your store. To keep up to date with Shopify trends and the newest advice, keep up with the ECommerce University *blog*, or even find a *meetup* or *networking* event, where you can meet and mingle with other Shopify users and swap tricks and tips.

Shopify Customer Support

Shopify offers support, 24 hours a day, 7 days a week. This is a major selling point, as when you're building and running your store, this will be your quickest, go to point of contact for immediate help. Shopify support is generally well regarded and considered competent and responsive.

Their support page, offering live chat, email, or telephone customer support, can be found here, http://docs.shopify.com/support. Shopify customer support can be contacted via live chat or email.

Both methods guarantee a fairly quick response and will put you in touch with a real human, in either case. Shopify also maintains a quick FAQ at their support site, in case you have a common question. The Shopify support page should be your next stop when trying to troubleshoot your Shopify account.

Get Your Shopify Trial – http://www.3stepwebsites.com/shopify-trial - Start your Shopify store with a 14-Day Free Trial.

Shopifybuilder.com offers Shopify development services on a for-hire basis, and is worth considering for a more boutique approach to building your Shopify store. However, they also maintain a great Shopify blog, which offers a lot of advice about Shopify itself and third-party apps and add-ons that can greatly enhance your Shopify store and owner experience.

My Online Selling Newsletter – http://bit.ly/1hAylMH - Sign up for occasional free tips, tricks, and updates pertinent to selling online and trending eCommerce strategies that I use within my own online stores.

Advanced Settings & Options to Optimize Your Shopify Store

Once you have mastered the basics of setting up your Shopify store, these advanced options will help bring a greater degree of professionalism and visibility to your store.

While they are not required to ensure the smooth operation of your store, these are strategies that will add advanced capability to your store in or der to increase your store's proficiency.

When you entered your domain name at signup, you were given a URL that looks like "your-shop-name.myshopify.com". Your myshopify account URL cannot be changed, but you can assign a different URL to your store. You can purchase a domain from Shopify, or assign your store a URL you already own.

Shopify hosts your site on their servers, so you don't have to worry about hosting your own site. It's a good idea to buy a professional sounding, easy to remember domain name.

Buying a URL

Shopify gives you the option to add a domain you already own (if, for example, you purchased one through GoDaddy, or another service), or buy a domain through your Shopify backend. Let's take a look at buying one through Shopify, first.

First, in your administrator panel, go to "Settings," then "Domains". In the header of the "Domains" page, in the upper-right, you'll see a blue "Buy Domain" button. Click it. The "Add A Domain" box will appear. Under "I want to…," select "Register a new domain name." Enter the domain you want to purchase in the field below. There will be a drop-down menu with extensions (.com, .co, .net, etc.), listed alongside their price. Now click "Check availability" to see if your domain is available. If the domain is available, a new box will appear, reading, "Register a New Domain Name."

Your contact information which you supplied to Shopify will be listed, and, under that, links to an ICAAN (Internet Company for Assigned Names and Numbers) agreement, and a domain registration agreement. Check the box, indicating you agree to the terms laid out, and click "Confirm purchase." Shopify will send you an email with some further steps to verify your purchase.

Check your email account associated with Shopify. An email from Shopify with the subject "VERIFICATION REQUIRED" should be in your inbox. Click the link that begins with "https://approve..." You'll be taken to another page to affirm more terms and conditions. Click "Submit," and you're good to go. Your newly purchased domain will be available in the "Domains" page of your administrative backend. In "Domain settings," the status of your new domain will have a check mark and an "OK" next to its name.

Add a Domain You Already Own

If you've bought a domain from a domain-registration service, Shopify allows you to set it as the domain for your store. For GoDaddy, BlueHost, Hover, NetworkSolutions, 1and1, Namecheap, and CrazyDomains, Shopify has special instructions for adding domains via those services.

We don't have room to detail each process, but detailed instructions from Shopify's help manual can be found here:

http://docs.shopify.com/manual/settings/domains/outside-provider

You will also find further instructions to add a domain you own through services not mentioned above, and steps to manage subdomains, as well.

Modifying Your Theme Using Theme Settings

Using Shopify's theme settings provides you a lot of control over the look and feel of your selected theme, without having to know code.

To modify your theme settings, go into your administrator panel and navigate to "Themes." In the "Themes" page, you'll see a list of published themes, with options for "Theme Settings" and "Template Editor." Click "Theme Settings" for the theme you wish to modify. (Although the box is labeled "Published Themes," you can also edit unpublished ones in "Theme Settings.")

From here, you have a couple of options. The "Preview in new window" button under "Live theme preview" allows you to preview changes in a new pop-up window. "Theme presets" allows you to toggle through the preset looks that came with your theme.

The meat of the "Themes" page, however, is the big list of options for customizing the look and function of your eCommerce website, including "Logo, Images and Colors," "Home Page," "Product Page," "Blog Page," and "Cart," among others. Each of these options is available via a collapsing menu. Any change you make will show up in your live preview, but changes aren't set until you hit "Save" in the upper right-hand corner.

Theme documentation is also available on top of the "Themes" page. This is all the necessary info you'll need in order to modify your theme. Each theme will have it's own customization options and instructions for doing so in this documentation.

It's highly recommended that before you modify your theme substantially, you duplicate/export a copy of the original theme so you can revert to it. We explain the process for doing so below.

Modifying Your Theme With The Template Editor

Once you've selected your theme, Shopify also lets you get into the code of the site (unless you're on their Starter Plan, which doesn't allow this ability). There's a theme settings editor or template editor that allows you to modify the HTML, CSS and other code elements, for instance swapping in links to your social media accounts, a step you'll want to take early on. Unless you're a skilled web designer or developer, it's best to go slow when making edits to your site; a little mistake could crash the whole thing.

We don't have room to offer you a comprehensive guide to editing code in a Shopify theme, but Shopify provides an introduction to the topic (http://docs.shopify.com/manual/configuration/store-customization).

However, the beauty of Shopify is that modifying your theme is not at all a necessity. In fact, you should spend time selecting the best theme for your store upfront, that way it encompasses everything you need and customization is not needed. If you can't find a theme that meets your needs, look to enlist a competent Shopify store designer to help you build your store.

Duplicating a Theme

Before you do any major modifying of a theme, you'll want to duplicate it. Shopify allows you 8 spaces for themes, so you shouldn't feel bashful about duplicating them.

Go to the "Themes" page in your admin, and find the theme you want to duplicate. In the lower right-hand corner of the theme's box within the "Themes" page. A new copy of your theme, as it was when you duplicated it, will be reproduced in the "Unpublished Themes" section. This is your fail-safe, in case you need to revert to an older version. You can also export it, which is certainly recommended.

Exporting a Theme

To store your theme locally on your own computer, you'll need to export it. This will allow you to modify it offline so changes won't affect your store. For most storeowners, it's good to export your theme just to have a copy if anything goes wrong with your store and you need a fresh copy of your theme to upload.

You can export themes by going into the "Themes" section of your admin, and heading to a theme's section in "Published" or "Unpublished" themes. Click the "Export" button at the bottom, and Shopify will send you an email at the address associated with your account with a download link to a .zip you can save locally to your own computer.

Shopify Mobile and Shopify POS (Point Of Sale) are both mobile, portable solutions to selling your Shopify products in real-world environments, while still incorporating sales, orders, and customer data into your online platform.

Shopify Mobile

Shopify Mobile (http://www.shopify.com/mobile) is an app, which you download to your smartphone. (While currently only available for iPhone, and Android version of the app is in development.) Once the app is installed, integrating it with your online store is quick and easy. If you have already signed up for a paid, Shopify Mobile is free with your subscription.

This includes a credit card reader that you physically attach to your iPhone to scan customers' credit cards on the spot. While the Shopify Mobile app does take a small percentage of each transaction, this is a great way to take your Shopify store products out into the real world and obtain in-person purchases, at places like trade shows and fairs.

Shopify POS

Shopify POS is essentially the iPad analog to Shopify Mobile. However, while the limitations of the Shopify Mobile app preclude its use in a store setting, or integration with further commerce devices, Shopify POS can be essentially be used as a fully functional cash register.

The Shopify POS card reader is provided by Shopify, and other products, such as a cash drawer, receipt printer, and item scanner can be purchased for an additional cost. Using the Shopify POS app as the basis of your pop-up store or newly opened shop can be a great low cost way of bringing together your in-person customers with those online. As with the Shopify Mobile app, the Shopify POS app will integrate all sales, orders, and customer information from online and in-person sales together.

Innovation within the eCommerce space is rapidly evolving, which is why Shopify has created an open source marketplace for developers to offer storeowners new functionalities for their stores in the form of apps.

Shopify apps provide you the ability to enhance your online store by adding new functionalities. Shopify offers the ultimate online store solution, but understands that other developers are better at creating certain functionalities. This gives you the best of both worlds. Shopify provides you with a powerful online store solution, and then you can tap into incredibly powerful applications depending on what you want to add to your store.

New apps are constantly being added to the app store, helping you enhance your store's marketing functionalities, provide advanced tracking/reporting, sync services for 3rd party applications, such as retargeting advertising, and much more.

Applications Overview

Every Shopify store will boast the same features and functions right out of the box. Adding applications to your store help you enhance your store in ways that are unique and important to your business.

Apps range in price from free to paid, with some of the paid apps costing a recurring, monthly charge to use for your store.

Shopify App Store & Installing Apps

You can search for exactly what you need in the Shopify App Store. You can enter in search keywords such as "email marketing" or "social media" or you can sort through the categories of Apps that Shopify lists on the homepage of the app store. You can even sort through apps based on price.

Installing apps couldn't get any easier. From within the Shopify App Store, simply find the app you would like to add and click the "Install App" button. Each app will then have it's own prompts as to how to use and what information it may need from you.

Applications that you've activated will be accessible from within your dashboard. Depending on what the app does, the admin settings for the app will be placed according to its function from within your dashboard. For example, applications that help you enhance your products' SEO will most likely place it's newly added functions to where you already edit your products SEO.

Let's explore a few apps that I highly recommend to all of my clients, enlist on my own stores, and are highly touted by the Shopify community.

The Best Shopify Apps for Your Store

Facebook Store

Facebook Store is an app that integrates your business's Facebook Page with Shopify. It turns a section of your store's Fan Page into a storefront, allowing you to sell products to customers right from your Facebook Page.

To install Facebook Store, navigate to the Shopify App Store, and search for "Facebook," or visit: https://apps.shopify.com/facebook-store

On this page, just click "Get App," and the installation process will start. You'll have to enter your Shopify store information, and then link the app with your *personal* Facebook page. Once the Facebook Store app syncs with your personal Facebook account, it will auto-detect which pages you administer, and ask which page you would like to sync with your Shopify store. Select your business's Facebook page.

After installation, Facebook Store can be accessed in your Shopify administrative backend. Here, you can customize the layout of your Facebook store and automatically update prices, product changes, and other information. You should use your Facebook Store to showcase some of your most popular and best-selling products, or those that you think will appear specifically to your Facebook audience.

The main goal will be to drive customers to your Shopify store, so you should think of Facebook Store both as a means of selling products, but also as a way to draw more traffic to your Shopify store.

From your administrative backend you will be able to specify which product collections you want to display on your Facebook

Store page. Ensure that these are some of the most eye-catching product collections and remember to check your Facebook page to make sure that photos are displaying correctly, as these will be the main draw to your page. Facebook store also allows you to "like-gate" your Facebook store.

This essentially restricts viewership only to individuals who have "liked" your business page on Facebook. The upside to this is that you will quickly generate more Likes on Facebook, as users will be forced to "like" your page before they can view your products. However, you also run the risk of limiting your audience a bit, as some people will be turned off at the prospect of being compelled to "like" your business page.

The upside to this app is obvious. Over 1 billion people use Facebook worldwide, and Facebook Store allows them to shop, or share product information with their friends in a way that will lead them directly to your Shopify store.

Facebook Store is a free app, it just isn't compatible with Facebook mobile at this time.

Perfect Audience Facebook Exchange Retargeting

When you visit Facebook, you'll notice that ads that you see are targeted to appear more relevant to you. Facebook has been doing this for years, and have really refined the process since its early days. Ads on Facebook can now be controlled by their native self-serve ad platform, which advertisers use to select criteria like age, interest and geographical location, or by Facebook's retargeting service.

"Retargeting" is the process where, when you visit one page, your cookies are tracked across the web, so ads relating to the first page are displayed when you visit another one, in this case Facebook. Facebook's name for this service on their platform is

Facebook Exchange. The only problem is that you can't access Facebook Exchange through the site's self-serve ads platform, so you need a third-party solution.

The company facilitating this ability to "retarget" those visitors who left your site is Perfect Audience. Their app will allow you to get to retarget visitors on Facebook through a much simpler process than most advertisers use. The Perfect Audience's Facebook Retargeting app is the name of the app.

When a user leaves your Shopify store without making a purchase, Perfect Audience's Facebook retargeting program shows them your ads when they are on Facebook. Ultimately, utilizing this app means you can get those who've visited your store already to come back and shop!

You must setup an account with Perfect Audience if you wish to utilize this Shopify App. You can sign up via their specific page for Shopify users here: https://www.perfectaudience.com/shopifyretargeting/

It will give you instructions for adding a code to your store's backend so you can begin to target visitors who come and leave. It's very easy to do, so you will be able to follow a few steps and set this up yourself.

Perfect Audience only charges you based on your ad's cost per impression (CPM), so you are only charged when your ad is appears in front of those who've already visited your store. This means that there are no setup or monthly fees, and you'll even get a 14-day free trial, which includes $60 worth of ad impressions.

Exit Offers

Cart abandonment is always a prevalent issue for all eCommerce entrepreneurs. According to a study published by web research company Baymard Institute, nearly 68% of eCommerce shopping carts are abandoned before purchase. That's right, a stunning 68% of your potential business is slipping away, even though customers wanted your product enough to add it their cart.

This is where Exit Offers comes into play; it's a seller's solution to cart abandonment and lost conversions.

Exit Offers tracks your user's cursor, and when they make a move to leave your page, they're presented with a pop-up offer for a discount, free shipping, or customer support. The app allows you to customize which offers you're pushing, and useful data to track recovered revenue from cart abandonment.

Exit Offers (http://apps.shopify.com/sticky-exit-offers) is available for a $10 a month fee, with a 14-day free trial.

Abandon App

If Exit Offers is the screwdriver of cart abandonment, then Abandon App is the Swiss Army Knife. While offering the same service, the ability to reconnect with a customer who has abandoned their order, Abandon App also allows you to customize emails which will be sent to the customer, reminding them of their uncompleted order.

Abandon App allows you to create an email offering the promotion you want your customer to receive when they abandon their cart. You select which promotion these visitors should receive, and Abandon App automatically does the rest. You can even stagger the timing of your emails, in case an immediate email seems too desperate. It's a Shopify owned and operated app, so it's also easy to install and you can access it from your Shopify dashboard.

Abandon App also tracks what are known as "ghost orders," orders which fail to show up in your "Today" administrative rundown, because they were either begun the previous day, or finalized they day after, giving you a more accurate performance snapshot at any given time.

Abandon App (http://apps.shopify.com/abandon-app) offers a range of pricing, from free plans to $99 a month

Chimpified

Chimpified is a Mailchimp integration app for Shopify. Mailchimp is an email marketing service, which allows you to collect emails of customers and prospective buyers. The app allows you to automatically add customers to Mailchimp lists, create email campaigns to market your store, and customize them to reflect buying behavior. Mailchimp is one of the easiest to use and most effective email marketing services available, so Shopify users looking to do some email marketing should get this free app.

To get started, you'll need to sign up for a free Mailchimp account and download the Chimpified app. The Chimpified website (https://chimpified.com) offers tutorials on how to integrate your Mailchimp account with the Chimpified app.

When a customer completes a purchase, they'll be given the option to opt into email messages from you. When they do, they'll automatically be added to your Mailchimp list by the app, under the heading "Shopify customers." Chimpified also adds links to your Shopify administrative backend, and gives you the ability to create custom emails via Mailchimp templates that are fully compatible with your Shopify data.

Chimpified will collect and relay marketing data by ECommerce 360, so you can better target certain shoppers with promotions and other special offers. Chimpified also collects customer data and sales, and plugs this into your Mailchimp reports, allowing you to assess ROI and general campaign effectiveness.

Finally, Chimpified is a great auto-responder tool, so if you need to automatically respond to customers, Chimpified has you covered. Auto-responders are a great way to provoke certain kinds of customer behavior. You can reward a first-time customer, ask for reviews or testimonials, or a host of promotional or customer relationship management tasks. Chimpified allows you to customize these emails as well, so that customers who exhibit certain buying behaviors, or those in a targeted geographic location, for instance, will receive automatic response emails.

Shopify allows only one Mailchimp list to be synced with one store, thus you will need to create new Mailchimp accounts if you plan on opening additional Shopify stores.

The Chimpifed App (http://apps.shopify.com/chimpified) is free to add your store.

Beyond Shopify – Advanced Marketing & Sales Strategies for Running a Profitable Online Store

Once your Shopify store is operating smoothly, capturing orders, and starting to attract visitors, you will likely begin analyzing various opportunities that could make your online venture a more efficient and profitable one.

Online marketing encompasses a vast wealth of strategies: everything from running paid advertisements, to using social media channels, to writing content for boosting your store's search engine optimization results. However, of all the possible marketing strategies storeowners could employ, only few have the ability to drastically improve sales and generate new customers.

To avoid a potential information overload, we will look at just these marketing and sales strategies. The majority of my clients' stores, and my stores as well, rely heavily on these few essential strategies for generating the bulk of our business.

Email marketing is the most effective, yet under utilized marketing method available to online storeowners. There is no other communication channel that offers such direct contact with past customers and building relationships with prospective customers.

Combined with Shopify's discount codes and promotional tools, email marketing can reap massive profits for most storeowners.

The majority of online storeowners, along with most website owners, struggle to keep visitors from leaving their site. Most online storeowners get disappointed when visitors leave their store without making a purchase.

For the majority of businesses, converting online visitors into customers is the main objective; there is nothing wrong with aiming to achieve this. However, most businesses struggle to convert 1% of visitors into customers. This means that 99 out of 100 visitors come and go without ever establishing communication or a relationship with the store/brand.

Storeowners should not be discouraged by this low conversion rate since these numbers are normal. Rather, they should look to address such low rates differently than most storeowners do.

By understanding that most visitors won't make a purchase on their initial visit, storeowners should make it a priority to get visitors to return to their store numerous times after their initial visit. It's no secret that retail businesses' main objective is to converting prospects into customers. However, with new visitors only converting to customers at a rate of 1%, at best, storeowners must change their approach for achieving this main objective.

And email marketing is one of the most effective ways for getting visitors to re-visit your online store AND make a purchase. Urging visitors to pull out their credit card and make a purchase from a store or brand they've never encountered is quite the uphill battle, hence the 1% conversion rates. New visitors should be catered to differently than your already established customers base.

Offer a simple 5% discount or future store credit for $5.00 in exchange for visitors providing you with their email. You get their contact information and they receive incentive to make a purchase from your store...it's a win, win situation.

Now, every time you have a new product or promotion to share, you will have a list of interested buyers, whom are already familiar with your brand, that you can email to get them to visit your store.

Build A Customer List

Shopify has partnered with Mailchimp, a high-powered email marketing company, to make it easy for storeowners to create email capture forms that can be placed strategically throughout the store. You can even have an email capture form appear as a popup form when first time visitors come to your website. It is normal for storeowners utilizing such email marketing forms to see anywhere from 15-30% of visitors submit their email.

Instead of generating just one sale from every 100 visitors to your store, you can easily initiate communication with 25 visitors (25% conversion rate) by capturing their email.

Of these 25 visitors, that can now be marketed to for as long as you are in business (and they don't unsubscribe from receiving your emails), you will most likely generate 2-5 sales, rather than just the 1 sale you'd normally see.

In future promotions and offerings to these email subscribers, you can expect conversion rates closer around 5%, as this is the norm for my clients' businesses as well as my own. Now, one simple email will generate more sales than getting 100 new visitors to come to your store. The ability to build a dependable, passionate customer base will help you sustain a long-term, profitable business.

Running Retargeting Ads to Bring Visitors Back to Your Store

In the previous chapter, we looked at a few Shopify Apps that could drastically improve your store's profitability. Aside from the Mailchimp app, which will help you build an email marketing list and campaign, the Perfect Audience App is the next best App to add to you store.

While some storeowners will and should use paid advertisement from the get go, the majority of smaller online retailers will most likely not be able to run profitable advertising campaigns due to incredible complexity and budgetary limitations.

Don't get me wrong; no other marketing/advertising solution is more effective in scaling up a business than paid advertising. If you can constantly spend $1 on advertising, which sees a return of $1.50, then nothing should stop you from spending $100 to make $150, or $1,000 to reap $1,500.

However, finding a profitable campaign, as such, is extremely difficult to do, even for the more advanced online marketers. There are so many variables involved that it takes hundreds or thousands of dollars to tweak your advertisements until they reach a break even or profitable position.

There is a form of paid advertising that almost always realizes a profitable return on investment, and these ads are referred to as "retargeting ads".

You have most likely seen "retargeting ads" directed at you when you are browsing the Internet. These ads may appear on Facebook or other websites and will be promoting a product or service of a website you have visited in the past. These ads may even acknowledge that you've been to their website and say something like, "Come back and finish your order and receive 20%

off" or "Get free shipping on your order if you purchase before January 15th".

Since visitors are already familiar with your brand, website, and offers, they are 200-400% more likely to click on your ads (according to Perfect Audience's Website). These return visitors will also be more likely to purchase from you the second time around, especially if you offer a discount or promotion in your ad.

Not only will you get more clicks and better conversions with your retargeting campaigns, but the cost of running these ads is a lot less expensive than regular paid advertisements. Because your ads are highly targeted and receive a better click through rate than regular ads, websites will show your ads more than others because they can see that your ads are better serving their audience (as determined by the higher percentage of visitors clicking on your ads).

So not only are you getting rewarded with highly targeted visitors who are more likely to purchase from you, but you are paying even less for these clicks than you normally would when running regular paid advertisements.

There truly is no downside to running "retargeting ads".

Shopify makes it easy to run these ads, even for those storeowners with no experience in paid advertising. Perfect Audience is the third-party retargeting solution that is easiest to use and pair with your Shopify store via their free app; you will only pay for the advertising, not the app itself.

Perfect Audience only charges you based on your ad's cost per impression (CPM), so you are only charged when your ad is appears in front of those who've already visited your store. This means that there are no setup or monthly fees, and you'll even get a 14-day free trial, which includes $60 worth of ad impressions.

You can create various retargeting campaigns from within your Perfect Audience dashboard depending on your goal.

For example, you may only want to target visitors that landed on a certain product's page, but that didn't make a purchase. Perfect Audience will walk you through how to set this up, and provide you with a simple code to add to your Shopify store.

You can learn the ins and outs of their platform by visiting here: http://support.perfectaudience.com/knowledgebase

Pro Tip
The one caveat with retargeting is that you must have visitors coming to your store already, otherwise there is nobody to retarget to with your ads. Regardless if you decide to run a retargeting campaign, set up the Perfect Audience App as soon as possible so it can begin to track all visitors to your store. It will begin to add all of these visitors to a list that you can retarget to in the future at your discretion.

Listing Products on the Amazon Marketplace to Boost Your Bottom Line

As discussed in the beginning chapters of this book, today's retailers now have the option of selling their inventory on third-party marketplaces such as Amazon or eBay. We've also discussed using Fulfillment by Amazon (FBA) as your solution for order fulfillment.

Ultimately, as an online retailer and business owner in general, your bottom line is priority number one, and running your own online store puts you in complete control of increasing your bottom line.

However, selling inventory on Amazon's third-party marketplace is too profitable to ignore. One of the easiest and most effective ways to boost your bottom line profits is to leverage the Amazon marketplace to increase sales.

It takes only a few minutes to setting up a Seller Account on Amazon, which you can learn how to do here: http://www.amazon.com/gp/seller-account/mm-product-page.html

Some entrepreneurs have created entire retailing empires solely by selling on Amazon, yet this is inherently risky because Amazon can change policies at or shut down your account without notice for the slightest policy infraction or mishap.

But...it's tough to ignore a multibillion-dollar marketplace that has hundreds of millions of customers with their credit cards on file ready to purchase your products in one click.

Selling Your Products on Amazon

Selling products via your Shopify store, and selling products on Amazon, are two entirely different operations. Neither platform restricts you, the retailer, from selling your inventory on the other's platform or from selling on both, and overall there are very few downsides to selling on both channels.

Getting started selling your products on Amazon is as easy as setting up an account.

Once your account is created, you have two options for selling products.

Create Your Own Product Listing

First, you can create your own product listings to appear in Amazon. If you have your own unique products, this is how you will list your products for sale. You could also create a product listing if you are reselling a product (not your own product) that does not already have a listing on Amazon. This is rarely the case, as 99% of products being sold at the retail level have had listings created for them. The third instance, in which you would create your own product listing, is if you plan on bundling items to create a unique offering.

For example, you may want to sell wireless headphones and batteries together as one product. This would allow you to create your own listing, granted that you take pictures and provide all pertinent information for your offering, which may include assigning a new UPC to this product.

Making your own listing will require providing product images, descriptions, and other types of information so Amazon can produce the listing. By creating your own listings, you can control how the listing appears and will be the only seller for the item unless other sellers begin to sell your product, which we will now examine.

Add Your Product to an Existing Listing

The second method for selling on Amazon occurs when you are looking to sell a product that other retailers are already selling. If this is the case, you will be able to find your product's already existing Amazon listing and add your inventory for sale to the listing. Buyers will then have the option as to which seller they purchase from, meaning you will be competing with other retailers when it comes to selling this product.

Depending on your inventory, you will be able to list your products for sale with any of the above-mentioned methods. The reason why we've touched on this aspect of selling on Amazon is because it impacts decisions that may affect your own Shopify store.

When you begin selling your inventory on Amazon, as well as on your own Shopify store, you will most likely run into at least these few questions:

What price(s) should I charge for my products?

Determining what prices to charge for your products should of course be based off your internal business figures, such as the price you are paying for the item, marketing costs, etc.

Once that is decided, there are several ways you can appoint prices across the various channels: price the products the same or charge a higher price on either your own store or on Amazon.

Every retailer should decide pricing based on their own business's needs. Consistent pricing across the board may be more important to retailers looking to build trust with their brands. Pricing higher on Amazon may make more sense for retailers looking to make up for the commission Amazon takes on every sale. For those retailers selling products with listings full of other sellers, pricing lower may be best as to be competitive.

My suggestion is to test different prices across both platforms, tracking results to see which pricing strategy works. Remember to consider the various fees associated with each sale (such as your payment processing, Amazon's commission, and fulfillment) when determining the best pricing fit.

Where should I send visitors or customers, to my own store or my Amazon listing?

Again, some business owners may differ in their approach here, but the answer is quite simple in my opinion. Since we are looking at building up our own business, and not Amazon's business, all traffic that we generate (ads, email marketing, social media, blogging, SEO) should be sent to our own Shopify store.

The main reason being that when someone purchases from our own store, they become our customer and not Amazon's customer. You collect the customer's email, address, payment information, and any other information you wish to collect when the sale is made from within your store. You can then market to these customers and turn them into repeat buyers via your email marketing efforts.

Amazon's marketplace should be used to supplement your business, not replace it. If you create a well-optimized product listing, or have products for resale that sell very well, Amazon does an incredible job of sending their own customers to your products' listings. All of these extra sales will bring in more revenue for your business, revenue from customers that you most likely will have never reached from your own marketing efforts.

Let Amazon put money in your pocket; just don't return the favor.

If you decide to sell your products on the Amazon marketplace, you will have the option to use Fulfillment by Amazon (FBA), Amazon's new fulfillment service, to fulfill orders placed on both Amazon or through your own Shopify store.

FBA is Amazon's relatively new third-party fulfillment service, offered to retailers looking for a warehouse and order fulfillment solution. Amazon extends this service to those retailers with an active Amazon Seller's account and whom sell on their website. In addition to syncing up with your Amazon Seller's account to fulfill orders, you can utilize their services to fulfill all orders placed on your own Shopify store.

FBA & Selling on Amazon

Using FBA provides several advantages to those selling on Amazon; these advantages include preferential treatment of your products' listings when they appear on Amazon.com.

According to an Amazon survey in 2013, "73% of FBA respondents reported that their Unit sales increased on Amazon.com more than 20%, since joining FBA".

Furthermore, your products will be eligible for all of Amazon's shipping options, including Amazon Prime, and Amazon will also take care of all of your returns and customer service. All of these factors combine to enhance your product listings on Amazon, which in return increases the amount of sales you make.

How Does FBA Work?

FBA is an all-inclusive fulfillment service that works in unison with your Amazon seller account (you must have an Amazon seller account to use FBA).

You send them your entire inventory, they store and manage your inventory, and then they will ship your inventory to buyers when something is purchased, all on your behalf – all you have to do is send Amazon all of your products.

Amazon even takes care of customer returns and customer service, simultaneously managing all of your inventory levels and revenue.

FBA & Selling on Shopify

If you opt to have Amazon do your fulfillment for your customers' orders via your Shopify Store, you will be employing FBA's multi-channel fulfillment feature. This feature is referred to as such because orders will be placed via a channel other than on Amazon's website, yet they will still fulfill the order.

You get to utilize Amazon's incredibly efficient order and fulfillment solution as if it were your own, giving your customers an incredibly seamless and fast-shipping experience.

To activate FBA from within Shopify, navigate to your administrative Settings, then to Shipping. Scroll to the Fulfillment services panel, and click "Activate," next to Amazon.

You'll then be redirected to your Amazon Seller account, where you should either login with your credentials, if they already exist, or sign up for a plan. If you are new to Amazon Seller, sign up for the "Sell as an Individual" plan. You must then manually set your shipping rates on Shopify, as described in the "Shipping" section, above, *such that they match Amazon's shipping rates.*

The next step is to go to your Products page, from your administrative main menu, and edit your Inventory & Variants settings. Here, you want to locate the "Fulfillment" drop down.

You should now see an option for "Fulfillment by Amazon." Select this option to sync this product with Fulfillment by Amazon. You must do this for every item that you would like to stock with FBA.

We've touched on the basics of FBA and the important takeaways. There is a lot more behind to Amazon's Fulfillment program, but as long as you understand what it is and how it benefits your business, you're on your way to become a profitable seller on Amazon.

Since this is such a new and powerful solution, combining your Shopify store with FBA, it's advised that you look over the most up-to-date information and instruction, which can be found here: http://docs.shopify.com/manual/settings/shipping/fulfillment-services#amazon

While the logistics for setting this up are important, it's only valuable if you understand how combining these two powerful eCommerce solutions can elevate your business's efficiency and scalability.

Saves Time

Instead of shipping every item sold, you just send your entire inventory to Amazon in bulk. They will sort your items and mark them as ready for sale. You don't have to deal directly with customers. All returns, shipping offerings, promotional rebates, etc. is handled by Amazon and can be tweaked by you in the backend.

Increased Profits

When you free up your time by eliminating routine tasks, such as order fulfillment and handling returns, you free up more time to focus on making other areas of your business more efficient.

More times than not, this leads to increases in revenue, which ultimately leads to increased profit.

How Much Does it Cost?

You are probably thinking that this FBA service must cost an arm and a leg. So did I, especially when my friend told me of all the headaches FBA had saved him. However, it's FREE to opt in to. That's right, FREE.

Once you have set up your seller account, you will have the option to enlist in this program. Any of the costs associated with FBA are variable costs, meaning you will only be charged for costs incurred once an item is sold. There are two costs that you will incur: monthly storage costs and fulfillment costs.

Storage costs: Currently it only costs $0.45/month per cubic sq. ft. to store your items with Amazon, with an increased rate of $0.60 during the holiday months.

Fulfillment costs: These costs vary for each product depending on the size, weight, and type of product and are charged to you only when a product is sold.

Both of these costs are standard costs for online sellers already, so you would be spending money on another fulfillment/warehouse solution anyways. Amazon is such an efficient company that these costs are drastically low compared to other solutions and even doing it oneself.

BONUS CHAPTER: Profitable Shopify Business Models that Require ZERO Inventory or Upstart Capital

This chapter covers three different types of online business models that anyone can execute while using Shopify as their online storefront AND without actually selling one's own products.

These opportunities will be most helpful to those looking for a completely new business opportunity, are new to selling online, or experienced online entrepreneurs looking to expand their online business.

Listed in order from easiest to hardest to execute, these three business models have been successfully executed by either my clients or within my own businesses.

Business Model 1: Online Arbitrage

This first business model, online arbitrage, is one that anyone can implement almost immediately. Although fairly simple to setup, this business model is very rarely used or even considered by most online entrepreneurs.

Online arbitrage is when you relist other online retailers' products for sale on your own online store at an increased price. When a visitor comes to your store and places an order for this product, you then turn around and purchase the product from the online retailer with the original listing at a lower price.

For example, an online pet store (we'll call them Store A) may offer a certain dog collar that your customers would most likely be interested in. They are charging $12 for the product, plus an additional $3 for shipping.

While you could go and buy that product in bulk or have it manufactured yourself, instead, you immediately make a listing for the product found on Store A and publish it to your Shopify storefront, as so visitors can view and purchase it.

You charge a premium price and list the same collar for $25 (with free shipping) because you've built a very appealing storefront and brand, specific to pet accessories. More times than not, visitors/customers won't mind paying a higher price if the perceived value is higher.

While some online buyers do thorough research and compare prices before making a purchase, the majority of online buyers prefers a quick, secure process with price taking a backseat.

Let's say 3 visitors place an order on your store for the dog collar. You have just made $75 in net revenue. You must now place an order from Store A for 3 dog collars, which costs your $45 ($12 x 3 collars + $3 x 3 for shipping). You have just made a net profit of $30, all without ever taking on any inventory.

You probably have a few questions at this point, such as:

- Won't customers know that the product didn't come from your store?
- What about returns?
- Won't the owner of Store A get upset and disallow you from doing this?

Well, the example certainly simplified the process, but let's address the above questions.

Won't customers know that the product didn't come from your store?

This question worries many of the storeowners interested in setting up an online arbitrage system. Before listing just any product, from any store, you will need to do some basic research and/or outreach.

First, make a list of products that would be great for your online store and that would interest your existing/potential pool of customers. Next, add to this list all of the stores carrying these products online. Make note of the price, shipping price and options, and other factors that may impact your ability to enlist arbitrage (e.g. there may be a minimum quantity you have to order). Last, find any contact email or number that would put you in touch with the storeowner, sales department, etc.

With your list complete, you can now contact the various stores to see which stores will work with you, using a template email like this:

Hi Storeowner,

I am in need of a product, similar to "x product" of yours, for an online store I run. Product x sell very well and fills a need that my customers have been looking for.

I wanted to know if I could run a test or set up a process where I list your product on my store, and then submit all collected orders to you for delivery?

My store is www.yourstoresurl.com and your product would complement our customer base perfectly. Please let me know if this would work for you, and if you have any further questions.

Thanks
Name

If you send this email out to enough stores, you will get a few positive responses and can begin to add their products to your store. With the relationship established, you can make sure that the business ships the product as a "gift" so their price/invoice does not appear in the package. Most storeowners I've worked with will go a step further and include my own invoice in the package that I have sent to them.

As for shipping, you can offer the same shipping options to your customers that the store you are working gives you (sometimes they will even give you better shipping rates if you end up generating a bunch of sales for them).

Pro Tip
For those looking to skip the outreach and/or relationship building process, and are looking to use online arbitrage as more of a way to test if certain products will sell, there's a way. Instead of committing to a certain supplier or business, you can usually find companies that allow you to have orders shipped without including an invoice (such as gift purchases) and/or can include

your contact details. You can even place an order yourself to see how it's packaged and delivered to you.

Additionally, many sellers on eBay and other marketplaces are use to customizing orders for such reasons, making them very useful for testing different products on your stores (plus the prices on Ebay are usually some of the cheapest, which means a better profit margin for you!)

What about returns?

Just like if you were to sell your own inventory, you must account for returns in your business. You can have a separate page on your Shopify store where you provide all return information, and throughout the order process you can simply state what your return policy is.

Assuming you allow returns, just provide your own address (not Store A's address) for returns to be shipped to. That's it.

It's then up to you to decide on how to handle your returns. You may be able to return the product to Store A depending on their policy and timeline of the whole return process, or you can relist for sale (depending on condition) and ship directly yourself to the next purchaser.

Won't the owner of Store A get upset and disallow you from doing this?

This is the question I get asked most, but should be the least of your concerns. Think about it. Why would Store A disallow you from giving them money?

Occasionally, a storeowner will get upset that you are charging more for their same product and won't do business with you. However, this has not been the normal reaction from any business owners I've approached when doing this. Most owners respond positively and look to further build on our business relationship by offering bulk discounts or reduced shipping rates.

Note
You must use common sense when doing this. Many big brands have a distribution system in place, requiring their approval to resell their products. You shouldn't be trying to sell Apple products for a premium – a) they are already premium priced products, and b) Apple will come after you.

Online arbitrage works best when selling generic type items that can be found everywhere. With so much competition for these types of products, retailers are looking to sell as many as possible and will give you the best prices possible.

Business Model 2: Drop Shipping

Similar to online arbitrage, drop shipping is the more commonly known business model where online arbitrage stems from. Drop shipping is the process in which a retailer markets/offers products that they do not actually have, and instead forwards orders to a company who does have the product to ship directly to their customer.

As you can see, this process is pretty much identical to online arbitrage.

However, I've distinguished these as two separate models because there are differences worth noting.

With online arbitrage, you are only re-listing products as found on other online stores and third-party marketplaces. Drop shipping differs because you are listing products from companies whom business is solely is drop shipping. These companies do not have their own online stores and aren't seen as competition; they generate all revenue by catering to the needs of other retailers.

You won't have to convince these companies to work with you as you would with online arbitrage. The more retailers they work with, the more money they make. While it is easy to establish relationships with various drop shippers, the process is certainly more formal. Many drop shippers have an approval process that you will have to go through.

They may want to see that you are already selling inventory or that your company has a resale permit or resellers license (every state calls it something differently and some states don't even require one). These licenses are very easy to get; your state government should have a well documented process on their website for getting one.

Where drop shipping makes up for it's lengthier process, is it's better pricing and broader product selection. With online arbitrage, you may be only able to mark up your products a small percentage as these other online stores are trying to maximize their profits as well. Additionally, your selection of products is limited to what products these stores are carrying, where drop shippers offer hundreds and thousands of products.

Additionally, since most drop shippers don't sell at the retail level themselves, they are ready to custom tailor completed orders to be sent to your customers. This eliminates almost all risk that your customers will receive their orders without your invoice and packaging specifications.

A quick Google search for "name of your product + drop shipping" will usually bring you back the businesses that offer drop shipping services for the exact product or entire product category you are in search of.

There are several online communities where hundreds and thousands of product suppliers/drop shipping companies offer their products to members. You can apply to join these online communities and once approved, you will have instant access to all of the suppliers and their products to sell on your own store.

Instead of applying to every supplier or drop shipping company directly, you can apply to just one of these communities. This will save you a lot of time and effort, and allows you to search the entire marketplace for the best products and prices.

Some of the best marketplaces/communities for getting access to drop shippers: www.dropshipdesign.com, www.doba.com, and www.dropshippers.com.

(I've personally used DOBA successfully to find a supplier that would drop ship for one of my electronics stores)

Pro Tip

Test some products on your store first with online arbitrage. The easiest way to do this is to message eBay sellers to see if they will be able to send my orders to your customers and exclude or customize their invoice for the order.

Once you start generating sales of a certain product, then start searching for a drop shipping company who will most likely offer better pricing, a better quality product, and additional products that may interest your customers.

Model 3: Selling Digital Products

Many online retailers and entrepreneurs are now in the business of selling information products such as eBooks, Apps, and online courses. These products, although lacking a physical presence, still must be able to be purchased and delivered to customers. Shopify has realized this trend and have ensured their platform is in a position to cater to such storeowners' needs.

This business model is one of my favorites because it truly does level the playing field for everyone looking to start a business. If you have a teachable skill, interest, passion, or information that others would love to have, you can start a business. You can create a digital eBook or record video tutorials that will cost you very little or nothing to produce, and then sell to anyone worldwide.

Many of today's most profitable online businesses are in the business of selling digital goods because once the product is created, there is no limit as to how many you can sell. It costs you nothing to "produce" another digital good, so every sale is almost 100% profit minus the costs of maintaining your store and acquiring a new customer.

FetchApp (http://www.fetchapp.com/) is a third-party service that you can use to host your digital product's file, and integrates with your Shopify cart, so that when customers purchase your digital goods, the transaction works seamlessly like any other Shopify purchase. The app will instantly deliver the digital good to the customer (think of it as a fulfillment service, just with digital goods).

FetchApp connects with your Shopify store via the FetchApp App (http://apps.shopify.com/fetchapp). While the app and it's functionality is free to deploy, the service is not; FetchApp offers variable pricing, depending on your storage and bandwidth needs.

Rates range from free to $500 a month. If you have a few eBooks or Video courses to host, you'll only need to enlist one of their inexpensive packages ($10/month) as it will be more than sufficient to deliver all of your orders.

To use Shopify and FetchApp together, you will download the FetchApp App to your Shopify store and then set up your FetchApp account.

You must first create the product listings for your digital goods from within Shopify so they appear in your store. Each digital good must has to have its own SKU, and the SKU for both Shopify and FetchApp have to match; every product variant must have its own SKU.

Now, from within FetchApp, after you've selected a desired account plan, it's time to upload all of your eBooks, video files, etc. Head to the products and payment page and activate Shopify from the carts and payment page.

Next, go to the products page and click the product import button. Upload the respective digital product to each product.

Testing a Digital Order

It's best if you make a purchase of the digital good from your Shopify store to test deployment by FetchApp. If set up correctly, you should receive a download email with a link to download your newly purchased product. If not, FetchApp offers support via its website. They have a user community and documentation for easy fixes, and you can contact them if there's anything that's not covered there.

Increase Your Store's Sales and Double Your Profits
...with my no-nonsense, simple-to-follow
Shopify Tips & Tricks

Delivered Right to your Inbox...for FREE!
Just visit - http://bit.ly/1hAylMH